W9-AXZ-011

614.4
Tur   Turner, Derek
4814⚹ The Black Death

THEN A
GENE
MAR

T

DE

Illus

WITHDRAWN

Alan N. Houghton Library
Renbrook School
2865 Albany Avenue
West Hartford, CT 06117

BLACK DEATH
TURNER DEREK   614.4 TUR   4814

LON

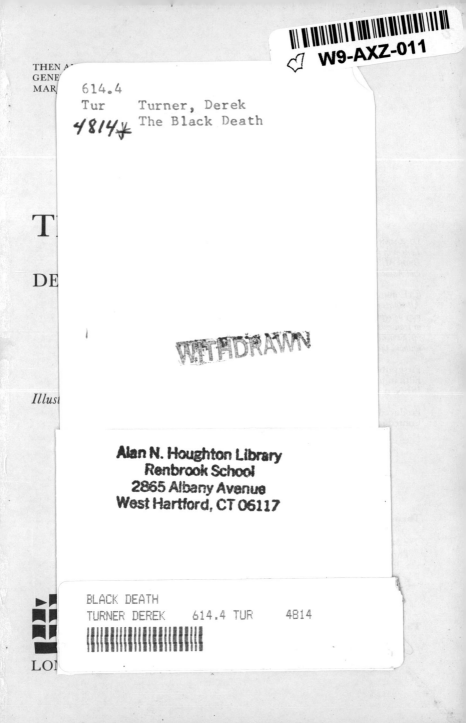

LONGMAN GROUP LIMITED
Longman House,
Burnt Mill, Harlow, Essex CM20 2JE, England
and Associated Companies throughout the World.

© Longman Group 1978
All rights reserved; no part of this publication
may be reproduced, stored in a retrieval system,
or transmitted in any form or by any means, electronic,
mechanical, photocopying, recording or otherwise,
without the prior written permission of the Publishers.

First published 1978
Fifth impression 1986
ISBN 0 582 20544 1

Produced by Longman Group (FE) Ltd
Printed in Hong Kong

Alan N. Houghton Library
Renbrook School
2865 Albany Avenue
West Hartford, CT 06117

4814

Then and There Filmstrips

The Medieval World, edited by Marjorie Reeves
Three filmstrips, in colour, with notes
1 Royalty, Knights, Castles, Tournaments, Religious Life
2 Country Life, Sports and Pastimes
3 Town Life, Home Life, Travel

Then and There Slides

Florence in the Time of the Medici, Marjorie Reeves

Contents

To the Reader

This book is about a fearful disease which suddenly struck Europe over six hundred years ago. It is a short story but a horror story. In many ways it is more of a picture in words than a story. A story has to be read from the beginning through to the end but when people come upon a picture they look first at whatever part most catches their eye and that part will look different to different people. This book is like a picture because I have described first those parts I find the most important. You or your teacher may decide however, when you have read the introduction, that you disagree with me about what is most important about the Black Death. You may feel for instance that what you want to know first is *why* the Black Death appeared in Europe. If so, you could begin by reading the last chapter. Unlike most books you will not lose anything by reading the chapters in the wrong order.

As the Black Death struck literally millions of people all over Europe, you will not get a complete picture of it from one small book. But when you have read all the chapters, in whatever order, you should have quite a clear idea of what the Black Death was, why it came, and the effects it had on the people of Europe.

Words printed in *italics* in the text are explained in the glossary on p.94

1   Introduction

The Black Death was the most terrifying thing that happened
to people in Europe in the *Middle Ages*, perhaps the most
frightening thing for a thousand years till the dropping of the
first atomic bomb. Terrible as that bomb was, only one city
suffered and death came quickly and suddenly; but the Black
Death killed hundreds of thousands of men, women and
children all over Europe. What made it even more frightening
was that it spread quite slowly. Kings, merchants, peasants,
doctors, all knew that it was coming and no one was able to
stop it.

You may have seen television reports of great earthquake
disasters in some far-away land, or of a serious plane crash
not so far away from your home. Pictures of these may have
shocked you, but imagine people in your own town or village
knowing that, perhaps next week, perhaps next month there
was going to be an aircrash or earthquake and there was
nothing they could do about it. Imagine knowing that in six
months time in your school class of thirty only twelve would
be left. Imagine yourself as one of the unlucky ones and you
may begin to get an idea of the effect the Black Death had on
people in the Middle Ages, whether they died or not.

The Black Death happened over six hundred years ago and
we shall never know exactly how many people died, nor precisely what happened in any one village, town or country. But it
is not so difficult to understand the feelings of people at the
time, to share the grief on Wednesday of a child whose father
had died on Monday and his mother on Tuesday. It is easy
to sympathise with those who tried to run away, to admire   5

those who stayed and tried to help the dying. I hope you will never have to face the kind of disaster that struck the people living in the fatal year of 1348 but it is no good pretending that something equally horrible could not happen to all of us in our lifetime. It could, and even if it was a much lesser disaster, like a car crash happening to one of your friends, studying and thinking about what the Black Death did to people could help you to understand what people feel and how they behave at bad moments in their lives.

In the following chapters you will discover what happened when the Black Death struck an ordinary family like your own and the sort of things that happened when whole cities and great areas of the countryside were affected, but first you will no doubt want to know what the Black Death was and where it came from. Early in 1348 when it first appeared in Europe people called it the plague. Only later was this first and most terrible attack of plague called the Black Death. People at the time had no real idea what kind of disease the plague was. Then, and until much later, any unpleasant and fatal disease which they did not recognise was called plague, diseases which doctors who are interested in history can now recognise as being something quite different, like typhoid. In 1348 the Italians, who were the first Europeans to catch the plague, knew that it came from somewhere in the East and was carried to Europe by ship. All sorts of strange ideas were put forward about what exactly caused the spread of the disease. At least, these ideas are strange to us. But if we remember that medieval doctors knew nothing about the plague, their most popular explanation was quite a sensible one. As the plague moved slowly from one region to another, people believed that the air was infected or poisoned and that this poisoned air was driven by the wind from one part of Europe to another. How the plague really spread you will find explained in Chapter 9.

But if no one really knew or could agree about what caused the plague to spread, everyone soon learnt what the symptoms were. A well known Italian writer called Boccaccio wrote

A medieval galley. This was the kind of ship most often used in the Mediterranean sea for trade and war. It was probably a ship of this sort that carried the plague to Europe

about the plague in his own city of Florence as follows:

> In men and women alike it first betrayed itself by the emergence of certain *tumours* in the groin or the armpits, some of which grew as large as a common apple, others as an egg, some more, some less, which the common folk called gavocciolo. From the two said parts of the body this deadly gavocciolo soon began *to propagate* and spread itself in all directions indifferently; after which the form of the *malady* began to change, black spots or *livid* making their appearance in many cases on the arm or the thigh or elsewhere, now few and large, now minute and numerous. And as the gavocciolo had been and still was an *infallible token* of approaching death, such also were these spots on whomsoever they shewed themselves....

Far away from the noisy city life of Florence, in the remote country of Wales the poet Gethin wrote of the plague like this:

> We see death coming into our midst like black smoke, a plague which cuts off the young, a rootless *phantom* which

has no mercy for fair *countenance*. Woe is me of the shilling in the arm-pit; it is *seething*, terrible, wherever it may come, a head that gives pain and causes a loud cry, a burden carried under the arms, a painful angry knob, a white lump. It is of the form of an apple, like the head of an onion, a small boil that spares no one. Great is its seething, like a burning cinder, a grievous thing of an ashy colour. It is an ugly *eruption* that comes with unseemly haste. They are similar to the seeds of the black peas, broken fragments of brittle sea-coal and crowds precede the end. It is a grievous ornament that breaks out in a rash. They are like a shower of peas, the early ornaments of black death, cinders of the peelings of the cockle weed, a mixed multitude, a black plague like halfpence, like berries. It is a grievous thing that they should be on a fair skin.

Modern doctors know that there were and are actually three slightly different forms of plague. The usual kind,

This writing was carved into the stone of Ashwell church in Herts. in 1350. It reads, in Latin, 'Wretched, terrible, destructive year; the remnants of the people alone remain'

described above, is called bubonic plague and it killed about seven out of every ten people who caught it, usually within seven days. But there were even more lethal versions; pneumonic plague in which the disease gets into the lungs and kills in two days, and septicaemic plague in which the disease enters the bloodstream and kills within a few hours. Both these versions of plague kill everyone who catches it.

Whatever the form, a worse disease than plague can hardly be imagined. Not only did nearly everyone die but the dying rapidly became disgusting masses of black or purple, decaying, stinking flesh. It was bad enough to have a mother dying before your eyes. To have her hour by hour becoming more *repulsive* was unbearable.

The plague was no respecter of persons. One king and several royal princes and princesses died. Wealth could not buy *immunity*. If you cut yourself off completely from others you had some chance of avoiding it—but then you would likely die of starvation. The Black Death killed rich and poor, strong and weak, saints and sinners but it was not a 'fair' disease. The poor suffered more than the rich. Some areas escaped lightly or got off entirely. In Italy the great city of Florence suffered terribly. In the equally powerful city of Milan far fewer died. Even more unfairly, in one small village some families would be almost wiped out, others would lose no one at all. Those who had the best chance of survival lived in small *hamlets* well off the beaten track. Those most likely to catch the disease lived in ports or in the big towns. In London for example, the plague, once lodged in the city, never completely left it for over three hundred years.

The end of the Black Death in 1350 was therefore not the end of the plague. There were a few cases every year and usually about once every ten years there was a serious *epidemic*. This went on until from about 1670 the plague vanished from Europe almost as suddenly as it had appeared. The *pandemic* was over. But for three centuries, from the mid-1300s to the mid-1600s, men were forced to face the threat of plague striking them and their families. They went on fearing it 9

This is an illustration from a book printed in London in 1625, which was one of the worst plague years in London's history

greatly and did anything they could to avoid it. The presence of plague brought out the best in some people, people like 'little Bess' who is recorded again and again nursing plague victims in Lancashire. More often it brought out the worst in people like those in Hertford who prayed that the plague would continue in London so that they would continue to profit from the presence of the royal court which had moved out to their town.

In the chapters which follow you will discover what happened when the plague struck particular families, villages and cities; how people behaved and how some managed to turn the plague to their advantage. These are only a few examples of many thousands, examples that we know of through some accidental survival of historical evidence. No two stories, no two tragedies would have been exactly alike but we can be pretty certain that the stories that have survived are not very different from the very many others that have been lost to history for ever.

2 *Plague Strikes Families*

Throughout Europe, literally millions of ordinary families were attacked by the Black Death, but the story of their misfortunes was never written down. Ordinary people could not write, and those few who could did not feel that the story of one family's troubles was worth writing down at a time when the whole world seemed to be littered with corpses. So all the stories in this chapter have been taken from later plague epidemics when people were better educated. But plague did not change over the centuries and you can be sure that stories very like these took place thousands of times over in 1348 and 1349.

At Great Hampden, a village in Buckinghamshire, not far from the town of Aylesbury, lived Robert Lenthall. He was parson of the village, and when anyone died in his *parish* he had to perform the burial service and also record their names in a register book. In his time he had no doubt conducted funerals where a tragic death had occurred, a young mother dying after childbirth, or a long waited for and much loved child, dead of pneumonia before his first birthday. Robert must have stood at the graveside of many of his good friends in the village. All sad occasions, but something a village parson had to expect as part of his job and learn to live with. But this year was different. People of all ages were dying thick and fast, the register bulging with new names, names of people who a week before were healthy and happy, friends and relations, all dying.

In a normal year Robert, as the law required, just noted down the names and dates of those he buried. But not this 11 year. Now the parish register was no longer just an impersonal official public record. For a brief time it became a private diary. Perhaps it helped Robert a little in his grief to write what he did. This is what he wrote:

My daughter Sarah Lenthall was buried the eleventh day of August [1647] she came from London to Whickham [High Wycombe] and on the Saturday only to see us and so to return the morrow in the afternoon to Whickam again, but then fell sick and on Wednesday morning following being the 11th of Aug. about an hour before sunrise died of the sickness and so in the evening we buried her in the *Mead* called the Kitchen-mead by the hedgeside as you go down into it on your left hand, a little below the pond at the entrance into the mead. She was aged 14 years eleven months and seventeen days—had she lived to Bartholomew day she had been full 15 years of age.

Susanna Lenthall my wife departed this life Thursday evening about eight a clock the 26 of August, she died of the sickness comfortably and in peace and was buried the 27 by [near] her daughter Sara.

John Gardiner a child that lived in my house died of the sickness and was buried August the 29th.

Adrian Lenthall my son, a hopeful young man and near one and twenty years departed this life of the sickness Thursday morning a little before daybreak and was buried at the head of his sister Sara's grave the same day, being the 2nd of September.

My cousin John Pickering, a lad about 13 years of age, dying of the sickness, was buried the 25 of September 1647.

Robert Lenthall, Rector.

Some hundred miles away in Kent, the Gale family was beginning to make its fortune, by working hard, saving money and gradually building up a flourishing blacksmith's business for goods made of iron were much in demand at the time. Lucky Francis Gale, head of the family, a large family with plenty of sons to carry on and expand the business! Lucky? Leonard Gale his son, writing in his old age takes up the story:

I was born in the parish of Sevenoake, in Kent, my father, a blacksmith, living in Riverhead Street, in the parish *aforesaid*, who lived there in very good *repute*, and drove a very good trade; his name Francis Gale: my mother was the daughter of one George Pratt, a very good *yeoman*, living at Chelsford, about five miles from Riverhead; my father had, by a former wife, two sons, and by my mother three sons and one daughter; and when I was between sixteen and seventeen years of age, my father and mother going to visit a friend at Sensom [Kemsing?], in the said county, took the plague, and quickly after they came home, my mother fell sick, and about six days after died, nobody thinking of such a disease. My father made a great burial for her, and *abundance* came to it, not fearing anything, and notwithstanding several women layd my mother forth, and no manner of clothes were taken out of the chamber when she died, yet not one person took the *distemper;* this I set down as a miracle. After her burial, we were all well one whole week, and a great many people frequented our house, and we our neighbours' houses, but at the week's end, in two days, fell sick my father, my eldest brother, my sister, and myself; and in three days after this my two younger brothers, Edward and John, fell sick, and though I was very ill, my father sent me to market to buy provisions, but before I came home it was noysed abroad that it was the plague, and as soon as I was come in adoors, they charged us to keep in, and set a strong watch over us, yet all this while no one took the distemper of or from us, and about the sixth day after they were taken three of them dyed in three hours, one after another and were all buryed in one grave and about two days after the two youngest died both together and were buryed in one grave. All this while I lay sick in another bed, and the tender looked every hour for my death, but it pleased God most miraculously to preserve me, and without any sore breaking, only I had a swelling in my groin, which it was long ere it sunk away, and I have been the worse for it ever since, and when I was recovered, I was shut up with two women, one man, and one child, for three months, and neither of them had the distemper.

This story had a happy ending for after a difficult two years when Leonard was down to the last £50 of the £200 he had inherited, things began to improve. When he died at the age of sixty-nine he left to his five children £16,000, a shop and a blacksmith's forge near Crawley in Sussex.

There is one unusual feature about Leonard's story which you may have noticed. His mother did not have the usual signs or symptoms of plague, the boils and the spots. We know from other accounts that this occasionally happened. Otherwise the plague took its usual and fatal course.

Both these families suffered heavy losses of life. Yet worse could happen. Some families, as you can read in the next chapter, were wiped out completely. Nevertheless the Lenthalls and the Gales were unluckier than most. The Deane family of Colyton, a large village in East Devon, was perhaps more typical.

Unlike Richard Lenthall, who was an educated man, and Francis Gale, who was a skilled craftsman, Edward Deane was an ordinary farm labourer. None of the Deanes wrote down their family story but we can piece some of it together from the parish register. The only unusual thing about Edward was that he was illegitimate and married Katharine, who was also illegitimate. He was also luckier than most in having eight children, six of whom lived to produce families of their own. We know nothing of his life outside the record of baptisms, marriages and burials but it is reasonable to guess that he died quite contented at the age of sixty-one. By this time, three of his children were married and he had six grandchildren growing up. His widow Katharine lived on, and at the age of seventy-three she was able to enjoy the sight of at least six children and no less than twenty-two grandchildren still living in the village.

Then, as at Hampden and Sevenoaks, the plague reached

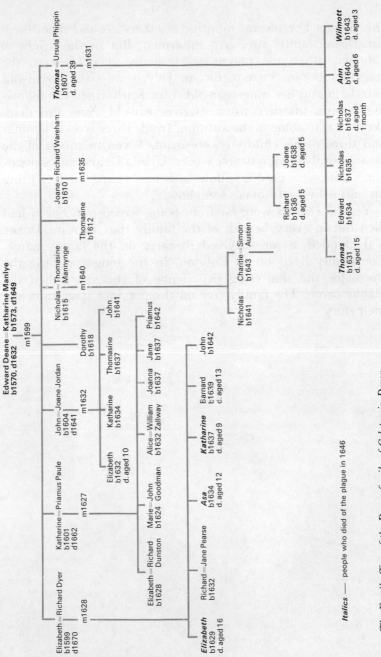

Edward Deane ═ Katharine Manlye
b1570, d1632   b1573, d1649
                m1599

Elizabeth ═ Richard Dyer
b1599
d1670
        m1628

Katharine ═ Priamus Paule
b1601
d1662
        m1627

John ═ Joane Jordan
b1604
d1641
        m1632

Nicholas ═ Thomasine Mannynge
b1615
        m1640

Thomasine
b1612

Joane ═ Richard Wareham
b1610
        m1635

Thomas ═ Ursula Phippin
b1607
d. aged 39
        m1631

Elizabeth ═ Richard Dunston
b1628

Marie ═ John Goodman
b1624

Elizabeth
b1632
d. aged 10

Katharine
b1634

Dorothy
b1618

John
b1641

Richard ═ Jane Pearse
b1629
d. aged 16
        b1632

Alice ═ William Zallway
b1632

Thomasine
b1637

Priamus
b1642

Charitie ═ Simon Austen
b1643

Richard
b1636
d. aged 5

Joane
b1638
d. aged 5

Edward
b1634

Nicholas
b1635

Thomas
b1631
d. aged 15

Nicholas
b1637
d. aged
1 month

Ann
b1640
d. aged 6

Wilmott
b1643
d. aged 3

Elizabeth
b1629
d. aged 16

Joanna
b1637

Jane
b1637

Barnard
b1639
d. aged 13

John
b1642

Katharine
b1637
d. aged 9

Asa
b1634
d. aged 12

Nicholas
b1641

Italics — people who died of the plague in 1646

The Family Tree of the Deane family of Colyton in Devon

15

the village. For several months, as others around them died, the Deane family survived unharmed. But in the height of summer, when the plague was usually at its fiercest, the tragedies began. First to die, in July, were sixteen-year-old Elizabeth and her nine-year-old sister Katharine. The following month, another sister, twelve-year-old Asa, also died. Worse was to come in the autumn. Inside three weeks, Thomas and three of his children were dead. Seven members of the Deane family died in twelve weeks. Ursula Deane, till September a wife, was now a widow with two young boys to bring up and a living to make somehow.

Yet the Deanes were far from being wiped out. Seven had died but in every branch of the family that Edward Deane had founded, a son survived to carry on the family name. The family lived on in Colyton, in the long run little the worse for the shattering experience of the year when the plague came. The family tree on the previous page sums up their story.

3 Plague Strikes the Countryside

The countryside of *medieval* Europe was divided up in two ways, into villages and *manors*. Often, but not always, the village with its surrounding fields covered exactly the same area of countryside as the manor. But even when this was so there was an important difference between them. A village was made up of a group of families living close together for various reasons. The site was sheltered against the prevailing wind, there was a water supply close by, fertile soil, a road near at hand, and so on. A manor, however, was someone's property and usually part of a larger estate. The whole thing was owned by one landlord. You probably think of an estate as a housing estate and a landlord as someone who owns a number of houses which he lets out to tenants, probably living in the largest and best house himself. In the Middle Ages, unlike today, houses were not particularly important or valuable. What made a man rich was owning farming land. So a medieval estate consisted of hundreds, perhaps thousands of acres of farming land. A medieval landlord was a man who kept the best farm for himself and let out the rest of his land to tenant farmers. Many villagers were therefore also tenants of the manor. What is more, unlike today, the tenants not only paid a rent in money for their farms, they also had to work for the landlord on his farm.

This difference between manors and villages is important because it makes a difference to what we know about the way the Black Death affected the countryside. A group of families living together in a convenient place and going about their ordinary life had little reason to write anything down, so there are hardly any records to tell us what happened in the villages during and after the Black Death. The manor on the other hand was a money-making business. How rich a landlord became depended partly on how well his land was farmed. If it did not make a profit he could not afford to live like a lord. Most landlords employed servants, *stewards*, *bailiffs* and *reeves*, to run the manor for them, and only by making them keep records could the lord find out whether the manor was making a profit and if his servants were cheating him. Hundreds of manorial records dating from the time of the Black Death still survive so we know a good deal about how many of the tenants died and whether the manor went on making a profit, but if we want to find a story of how a village suffered from the plague we must take it from one of the later plague epidemics.

The story of the plague in Eyam is quite famous. It has even been turned into a television play. The Eyam plague

An aerial photograph of the deserted village of Ingarsby in Leicestershire. Faint marks in the fields around the surviving buildings show where the village buildings used to be. There are written records to show that this village was deserted very soon after the Black Death. This does not mean that everyone in the village died of plague. Those who survived probably moved to another village to take over empty cottages and vacant lands

is famous, partly because it was very severe, partly because the story was told in great detail, nearly two hundred years after it had happened, by a man called Wood. He pieced the story together from written sources; the letters the village parson wrote and the parish register. He also used accounts of the plague told and retold by the descendants of those who survived and to these he added his own lively imagination. The story as he told it is dramatic but not always accurate. The version of the story told here is mainly based on what a modern scholar has discovered by taking a new look at the written evidence that remains. Certainly what happened at Eyam was most unusual in the seventeenth century. We really do not know for certain whether something like what happened in Eyam in 1666 also happened in many villages in 1348 but we do know that the disease was the same and that in some villages the proportion of people who died during the epidemic was the same as at Eyam.

Eyam is a village lying in the Derbyshire hills about ten miles from Sheffield. Just before the plague appeared the village consisted of about one hundred houses and something like 450 people. But if we include those who lived in small

The church of Eyam

An old print showing what the village street of Eyam probably looked like in 1666

hamlets or single farms outside the village there were altogether about 260 families living in Eyam parish.

The plague arrived in Eyam on 2 September 1665, when George Vicars unpacked a box of plague-infected clothes from London. He very quickly caught the plague and died after four days. At least, that is Wood's version of the story but it may have been brought by one of the large number of visitors from nearby Derby to the Eyam *wakes*, a yearly day of merrymaking, which took place on 20 August. But we are not certain that there was plague in Derby so cannot be sure how the Eyam plague started.

The first attack of plague was not so serious. Plague was seldom so active in the winter months and often disappeared altogether when the weather turned cold. But not at Eyam. Between 6 September and 31 December forty-six people in the parish had already died. Normally between twenty and twenty-five people died in the whole year. Some families had already suffered badly. William Rowe, his wife Mary and their baby all died in the fortnight before Christmas. William Rowbotham and his three sons were already dead, one buried on Christmas Eve and two on New Year's Day. In the later part of the winter and the spring there were few deaths from plague and the people of Eyam must have hoped that the worst was over, but in May the second and far worse attack began, lasting right through the summer and on into the autumn. By October about ninety of the 260 families had suffered a death and some 250 people lay in their graves.

Men and women died in about equal numbers. It was children and teenagers who were worst hit. Old people were hardly affected. Families suffered very differently. In about forty-five families one or at most two people died and in 170 families no one at all was lost. But in the Morton family there died, in the space of five weeks, father and mother and no less than nine children. Those living in the small hamlets and single farms were on the whole the luckiest. In the village things were far worse. When the second attack of plague started in May a few of the wealthier inhabitants fled. 'Some few others', says Wood, 'having *means*, fled to the neighbouring hills and there erected huts and dwelled therein until the approach of winter.' Then the parson, William Mompesson, fearing that those who fled would spread the plague to other villages, told the villagers that they must not on any account leave the village. Because they respected their parson the people did what they were told and Eyam village was cut off from the rest of the world. Any food brought from outside was left on the edge of the village and collected later by the villagers. The money to pay for it was placed in springs or troughs of running water, though the local lord, the Earl of Chatsworth, taking pity on the wretched people, provided much of their food free. The parson's actions were well meant but disastrous. Huddled in the village, unable to flee, the inhabitants suffered terribly. The Thornleys, the Yellotts and thirteen or fourteen other families were wiped out completely. In another fifteen both parents died. Only about half the village families managed to get through that terrible summer without a death.

With the plague surrounding them on all sides and the numbers of corpses growing every day, the remaining villagers lived on as best they could under William Mompesson's 21

The burial ground of one family struck by the plague. The village graveyard was too small for all the new graves that had to be dug and people feared to bury plague victims in the centre of the village in case the bodies spread the infection. So special burial grounds were made in the fields

leadership. The church and the churchyard were closed but services were held in the open with the congregation sitting spread out over the hillside. The corpses were buried in the fields and gardens, but there were too many to hold a proper burial service for each. As more and more people died and still the plague showed no sign of disappearing, the villagers, according to Wood, became divided against themselves. Those at the western end of the village shut themselves up in their houses and refused to cross the small stream which divided them from the rest of the village. By October over two hundred people, half the villagers, were dead and then at last the record of plague burials in the register stops. Those who were left, the young widows, the orphans, the aged and lonely, carrying a great burden of grief, now had to face the future.

The question we now have to consider is: was the story of most English villages and manors in 1349 like that of Eyam in 1666? If we read what the writers of the time, or chroniclers, say, it would seem that the answer is yes. One chronicler

writes:

'In the year of Our Lord 1349 the hand of God struck the human race with a certain deadly blow which, beginning in the southern regions, passed into the northern. This *scourge* in many places left less than a fifth part of the population living.' Another chronicler, Henry Knighton, writing at Leicester, goes into more detail.

In this same year a great number of sheep died throughout the whole country, so much so that in one field alone more than five thousand sheep were slain. Their bodies were so *corrupted* by the plague that neither beast nor bird would touch them. The price of every *commodity* fell heavily since, because of their fear of death, men seemed to have lost their interest in wealth or worldly goods. Sheep and cattle were left to wander through the fields and among the standing crops since there was no one to drive them off or collect them; for want of people to look after them they died in untold numbers in the hedgerows and ditches all over the country. So few servants and labourers were left that nobody knew where to turn for help. The following autumn it was not possible to get a harvester except by paying eightpence a day with food included. Because of this many crops were left to rot in the fields. However, in the year of the pestilence, these

Peasants burning the clothes of plague victims. People thought that the clothes of a plague victim would be infected with the disease

crops were so abundant that no one cared whether they were wasted or not.

All this sounds very convincing, but we must be careful. Chroniclers, like some modern newspaper reporters, liked to exaggerate or pick on the worst examples to make a more dramatic story. We need to check these stories where we can. Thanks to the many surviving manorial records we can do this. Henry Knighton for instance writes that prices went down and wages up, but look at this table of prices taken from a number of manors in Hampshire and Somerset. The price of wheat does go down a little during the plague but it soon goes up again. The changes in price are no greater than in any period of eight or ten years.

The price of wheat during the Black Death

Years	Price per quarter (28 lb) varied between
1347–48	5s (25p) and 8s 8d (43½p)
1348–49*	3s 6d (17½p) and 6s (30p)
1349–50*	6s 8d (33½p) and 9s (45p)
1351–52	14s (70p)
1355	5s (25p) and 8s (40p)

*plague years

Wages of farmworkers and craftsmen during the Black Death

Years	For every acre (4047 sq. metres) reaped	For every quarter of corn threshed	Carpenter's daily wage
1346–47	6 or 7 pence	2 pence	4 pence
1349–50*	4½ to 6¾ pence	2 pence	not known
1353–54	8 pence	2 pence	3 pence

*plague years

Wages are given in old pence: 2½ old pence = 1p

The main job in harvesting was cutting, or reaping, the corn. Notice in the figures given that in 1349/50 the reapers actually received slightly less than in the previous year. However accurately Henry Knighton was describing the situation in Leicestershire, things were happening very differently in the manors of Hampshire and Somerset. You would expect differences in different parts of the country, but were things the same for all the villages and manors within one region? To answer this question, we must look at two manors which are not very far apart, one in Oxfordshire, the other just across the county border in Berkshire.

Witney today is a busy market town not far from Oxford, famous for the making of blankets. In 1348 the manor of Witney was part of the very large estates of the Bishop of Winchester. The town itself was not part of the manor, which consisted of three small villages or hamlets; Crawley, Curbridge and Hailey. In Domesday Book, made in the year 1086, forty-seven tenants of various kinds are recorded. About two hundred years later, according to another similar survey, the number of tenants had grown to 114. The population of England as a whole is believed to have started to fall about the year 1300. This is certainly true of these villages where, by the 1340s, the number of tenants had fallen to between

Peasants reaping the corn under the eye of a harvestman

eighty and ninety. Of course there were more people in the manor than that. A tenant farmer would be helped by his wife and children and perhaps other brothers. He might well be looking after his aged mother. On average there were for every tenant about four others living on the manor. In addition a number of people would be employed on the lord's farm, or *demesne*, and there would be a few special tenants, craftsmen like the millers. In 1348 most of the tenants paid a yearly rent of five shillings and had to work for three days a week on the demesne. In addition, there were various special duties, the most important of which was getting in the lord's harvest. When the corn was ready, not only the tenants but almost all the men of the manor were expected to come and harvest it.

In the 1340s the demesnes of the three villages were doing quite well. Altogether just under 300 *acres* of corn were sown. There were forty or more oxen to draw the ploughs and about 700 sheep. In the years before 1348 the lord could expect to make a profit of about £30 per year from his farms and receive about £90 a year from his tenants. Then came the Black Death. For the year 1349 a new heading appears in the manorial records: *Defectus per Pestilentiam*—rents unpaid because of plague. Under this heading are written statements like this:

> 2s 6d [12½p] for the rent of one messuage [house and garden] and one *virgate* [thirty acres] of Walter le Kene, because the said Walter is dead and there is no one who wishes to take the said land and there is nothing from which the said rent can be paid.

No less than fifty-nine tenants, about two-thirds, died during the year and very few tenants could be found to replace them. In 1350 there were still forty-five unfilled tenancies though some were temporarily let for the reduced rent of 3s [15p] per year. No one could be found to take over one of the three mills so a further £8 of rent was lost. The profits of the farms fell to £3 in 1349 and £4 in 1350. The large number of deaths helped to balance this because when a tenant died a tax in money or goods called a fine or *heriot* was paid to the lord from his property. So in 1349 the lord received £30 in fines. Nevertheless the whole profit from the manor in 1349 was only half of what it had been the year before. In the next few years things got worse rather than better. Look at the graph and you will see this. Gradually a few more tenants came forward but only on condition that they did not have

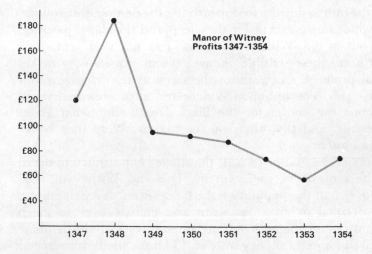

Manor of Witney
Profits 1347-1354

to work on the lord's farm. As a result the lord for the first time had to start paying people to work for him as you will see from the following figures.

Year	Number of people who came to harvest (unpaid)	Money paid in wages to reapers
1348	121	none
1349	60	£3.10s (£3.50)
1350	28	£5.10s (£5.50)

It soon became clear to the lord that he had to make changes if this manor were to start making a decent profit again. If we jump in time to 1376 we can see the changes that had been made. The tenants' rents have been put up a little from five shillings to six shillings and eightpence. No tenant has to work on the lord's demesne any more but they have to pay not to work on it! Only 164 acres of corn have been sown, about half the former amount. The bishop is now making his money from stock farming, that is breeding and selling cows and sheep, particularly the latter. The number of sheep on the farm has doubled from about 700 to 1485. Finally in 1377 the bishop decides to stop farming the demesne altogether. The whole farm, except for the sheep and the sheep pastures, is let out to one William Gilles for £11 per year rent. As a result of all these sensible changes the manor in 1377 makes a total profit of £115, about the same as the average profit in the 1340s. The Bishop of Winchester, after a few bad years, was none the poorer for the Black Death. But what about the tenants and the others on the manor. Were they better or worse off?

Many of the manor records that have been studied in detail tell the same story as Eyam in 1666 and Witney in 1348 Well over half the population died, tenancies were left empty, lords decided to grow less corn and change over to sheep farming and no longer demanded unpaid work on the demesne but asked for extra money instead. (This is called *commutation*.) Some historians immediately decided that this is what happened all over the English countryside. How wrong they were we can see by turning to look at the manor of Brightwell.

Brightwell was a manor like Witney in several ways. It too belonged to the Bishop of Winchester. It also contained three small villages and lay about the same distance from Oxford. It was a little smaller, with about sixty-six tenants, perhaps 400 people altogether in the 1340s. The annual profit from the demesne and the rents amounted to about £80. When the Black Death arrived, only nineteen tenants died, less than a third, and all were replaced within two years, apparently without any difficulty. The profit of the manor dropped much less. Look at the graph and compare it with the graph for Witney. From the lord's point of view, the death of perhaps 28 a hundred people from the Black Death made very little

An aerial view of Brightwell Baldwin today, one of the three villages of Brightwell manor. The big manor house in the centre of the picture was built later but otherwise the shape and size of the village has changed little since 1348

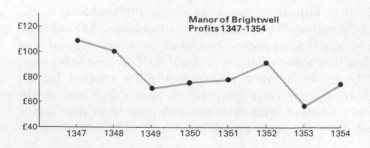

difference to the manor. The position of the tenants did not change very much either. In 1377 many were still forced to work unpaid on the demesne, and where they had managed to commute their labour it cost them much more than at Witney, between 9s (45p) and 13s 4d (66½p) for the usual thirty-acre farm. The people of Brightwell manor certainly suffered much less than those of Witney at the time when the Black Death raged but in the long run they were not better off.

In one important change Brightwell was like Witney. By 1377 the number of acres of corn sown had dropped from about 160 to just over 100 acres. This could have been because, as at Witney, there were not enough people to plough and reap or, more likely, because the bishop found little profit in selling corn now that there were fewer people in England to eat it.

There is no record of any sheep on the manor of Brightwell, either before the Black Death or later, but on several other manors in the neighbourhood, the number of sheep grew only slowly, if at all. Nor was the amount of corn grown always reduced. In fact, the more manors we study, even manors that were part of the same estate, the more differences we find in what happened. You should now be able to understand why historians believe that what Henry Knighton wrote was not the whole truth. Perhaps you can also understand why historians find it difficult to agree among themselves about what the effects of the Black Death were on the English or European countryside as a whole.

But we should not end this chapter thinking about the problems of historians, nor even about the problems of the lord of the manor. We should think rather about the problems, and perhaps new opportunities, that faced the tenants and their families: about what a wife could do if her tenant husband died; how the ordinary people would be affected by the change-over from corn growing to sheep farming on the demesne; whether tenants really did gain from not having 30 to work on the demesne any more; about what would happen if one manor were badly hit by the Black Death and another, a few miles away got off much more lightly.

In some villages we can find out what happened to the ordinary villagers once the Black Death had come and gone. For instance in three villages in the Lincolnshire fens where over half the tenants died we know who took their place. They can be summarised as follows:

Children of the previous tenants	21
Wives of the previous tenants	8
Other relations	7
Others, not related to the previous tenant	36

In half the farms there was no one from the family to take over. Perhaps they had all died or perhaps the children were too young or their mother too old or too ill. What then? Manorial records can only tell us a part of what actually happened in a cold, unemotional way. We have to use our imagination, our feelings and our brains to fill in the gaps. The historian Edward Jessop put it this way:

A man's whole household may have been swept off— young and old, babe and *suckling*, sister and brother, and aged mother, and wife, and children, and servant, and friend—every soul of them involved in one hideous *calamity*. The steward of the manor was not concerned with any but the head of the house—the tenant of the manor. Was he missing? Then, who was his heir? Any sons? Dead of the plague! Brothers? Dead of the plague! Children? Kinsfolk? All gone! Their blackening carcases huddled in *sweltering* masses of *putrefaction* in the wretched *hovels* while the pitiless July sun blazed overhead.

The steward made his entry of one fact only. Thus:

The Jurors do present that Simon Must died possessed of a *messuage* and four acres of land in Stradset, and that he has no heir. Therefore it is fitting that the aforesaid land be taken into the hands of the lord.

Also that Matilda Stile—was she married or single, widow or mother or maid? What cared the precise man of business 31

on that 24th July 1349, as his pen moved over the *parchment*?
—'Matilda Stile died possessed of one acre and one *rood* of land. Therefore it is fitting that the aforesaid land be taken into the hands of the lord until such time as the heir may appear in court.'

He never did appear! Next year her little estate was handed over to another. She was the last of her line.

After looking at what happened in many different places over England, historians have decided that the Black Death was a disaster for some but a blessing in disguise for others. Many families suffered disaster but many others were able to start building up their fortunes by renting or buying land cheaply. Some families were turned out of their homes to make way for the great new sheep pastures that the lords made in parts of England, but there were new opportunities for families to make a good living by becoming weavers of woollen cloth. Hard-working and go-ahead tenants found that it suited them to pay a money rent for their land instead of working on their lord's farm because, with fewer workers about, wages went up. A man who worked hard could pay his rent and still have money left over to rent more land or buy a few luxuries for himself and his family. Quite often those who were living on poor land or had a bad landlord could do better for their families by moving to another village which had been badly hit by the Black Death. Before 1348 most ordinary people had about the same amount of land and wealth. After the Black Death there came to be less equality but more opportunity. Many, through bad luck or bad management, got poorer. Others, who were lucky, hard-working, ambitious or clever became richer. We will consider in Chapter 7 whether all these changes, opportunities to move to a new village and to become richer, actually made people happier and more contented.

4 *The Black Death Strikes a City: Orvieto*

If you had been a medieval pilgrim on your way to Rome in the 1340s you would almost certainly have stayed the last but one night of your journey in the city of Orvieto, a convenient stopping place on the main road about sixty miles (96 km) from Rome. As you climbed with your tired horse up the steep and winding road, you would have seen the city, perched on

A modern photograph of Orvieto cathedral. Notice how grand and highly decorated the front of the cathedral is. Only a town with wealthy merchants could afford to put up such a building. In the 1800s the rich men of the industrial towns, like Manchester for example, usually built grand town halls. Today it is more likely to be shopping or recreation centres

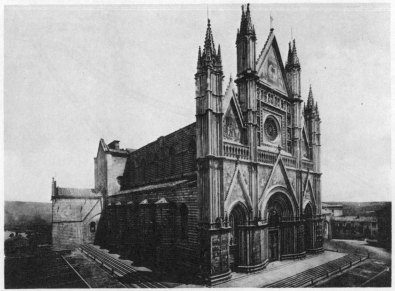

33

its high rock, its towers standing out against the blue of the sky. When you finally reached the Porta Rocca (one of the main gates) you would no doubt have paused to get your breath back and gaze at the valley 600 feet (183 m) below. Then, as you made your way on down the Via Postierla and into the the open square called the Piazza del Vescovo, you would no doubt have been impressed by this busy city with its fine cathedral, brand new and not quite finished, which dominated the square. With sharp eyes, however, you might have noticed on your right as you came in some ruined houses in the Santa Pace quarter, houses destroyed, as a local could have told you, when one party of nobles was forced out of the town after one of the frequent quarrels within the city. In fact you might have been so unlucky as to arrive in the middle of one of the battles between the armies of Benedetto

Map of the town of Orvieto as it was in 1348

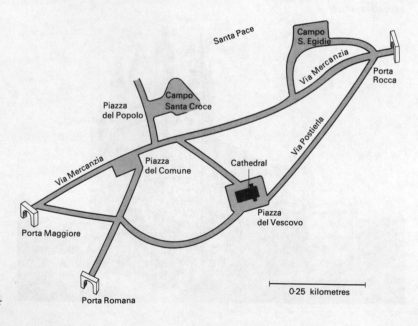

de Bonconte and the Monaldeschi family which were raging in 1346.

But if you had been a Roman merchant stopping off on your way home from Florence with a load of the latest fashion cloth, you would hardly have given a second glance at Orvieto, for in many ways it was a typical small Italian city. There

Map of Central Italy showing the main roads

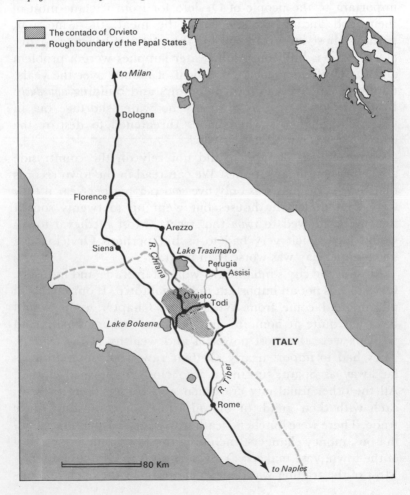

were several like it in Umbria and Tuscany: Siena, Perugia, Assisi. Orvieto was part of the papal states, that is lands that were ruled by the Pope of Rome. 'Of' Rome, not 'at' Rome, because at this time the popes were living far away in Avignon in the south of France and the papal states were poorly ruled.

In fact Orvieto really governed itself and also its *contado*, that is the countryside which surrounded it, about the size of a small English county. The contado was very important to the people of Orvieto for from it came most of their food and drink; the corn, the meat, the wine and, perhaps most important of all, the water. Orvieto is a dry place. As it is built on a hill, water supplies were a problem and the city had spent a great deal of money over the years, damming up rivers to form reservoirs and building *aqueducts*. By the 1350s there was normally no water shortage but in years of drought or when floods threatened to destroy the dams, life was not so easy.

Some citizens of Orvieto did not rely on the countryside alone for their meat supplies. We can read in the town records that the tax on pigs was only five *sous* per pig per year if they were kept under the houses but went up to twenty sous if they were allowed to *roam* the streets. Most medieval towns would have smelt very bad to us but perhaps Orvieto on a hot summer day was worse than most.

Most of the city's inhabitants worked in trade and industry. Orvieto was not an important industrial town. If our medieval pilgrim had come from Witney (see Chapter 3) he would have felt quite at home to find that its wool merchants and weavers were the most powerful and wealthy of the traders. They had to import nearly all their raw wool, some from as far away as Spain, turning it into cloth or finished clothes. All the other usual city craftsmen and traders were present, each with their guild, or organisation, for controlling their trade. There were butchers, leather workers, carpenters, stone-masons, money changers (including the Jews), and a speciality of the town, vase makers. (You can still buy Orvieto pottery.)

Most of the trading was done in shops or in the open marketplaces. Every year in September was held the great fair of St. Severo, the patron saint of the great abbey nearby. Then merchants would flock in from all over Italy and even further away to buy and sell wholesale. They overflowed from the two main market squares of the Piazza del Popolo and the Piazza del Comune into the open spaces of the Campo de Santa Egidie and Santa Croce where the cattle market took

A street in the town of Bologna in Italy in the Middle Ages. The shopping streets in Orvieto would have looked something like this

place. The city took a rake-off of everything that was sold and this market was one of its most important sources of money. Because Orvieto was on or near a number of roads, it was a convenient meeting place for outsiders to come and sell their goods to each other. If the citizens had been forced to rely for cash only on what they themselves made and sold, they could not have afforded to import the luxury goods they liked, such as gold jewellery from Venice, gold-embroidered cloth from Florence, *serge* from Ireland, spices from the East. Most of the citizens of Orvieto were used to living well. Richest of all were the nobles. Their wealth came not from trade but from the large estates they owned. The laws of the city did not allow them to trade and they were forced to spend a good part of the year living in their town houses rather than in their country mansions. There was great rivalry between different groups of noble families and their town houses grew more and more like fortified sky-scrapers.

A modern photograph of San Gimignano, a small town in the same part of Italy as Orvieto, where a large number of the medieval towers still survive

It was not only a question of 'keeping up with the Joneses'. One had to be able literally to look down on them!

The leading merchants were almost as rich as the nobles and had almost as much power in running the town. The people who ruled changed often in all Italian towns. Originally most cities were ruled by the nobles. Then the merchants' power grew and they took over the leadership. Because of the many quarrels between leading local families, the governorship of the town was often handed over to an outsider, called a 'podesta'. In time the ordinary townspeople came to hate the rule of a single man and they chose their own representatives to govern the city. These in turn were challenged for power by particular noble and merchant families. In times of crisis in Orvieto a group of four men called the 'balia' was given emergency powers. The mid 1340s was one of these periods of political crisis. The peace and independence of the town was being destroyed by the soldiers of the local noble families like the Monaldeschi and the army of the rector, or governor, of the papal states, Benedetto de Bonconte, and his allies, including the town of Perugia.

In 1346 it was difficult to know who did in fact rule the town. Power was shared between the podesta, an officer called 'the captain of the people', and the balia. Between them they carried out the laws, but the laws themselves were passed by two councils: the 'council of seven' (actually consisting of eight people) and the 'council of forty'.

In spite of all its complicated politics, Orvieto in 1346 was quite a happy and prosperous place. There were only 15,000 inhabitants, compared with Florence's 90,000, but it was able to do well from its good position on the busy trade routes. The richer citizens could afford their luxuries because of the trade outsiders carried on in the town. The ordinary townspeople lived a comfortable life because the surrounding countryside provided them with most of what they needed, bread, meat, wine and water. It was an easy life—but it could easily disappear. If for any reason country supplies from the contado dried up or outsiders stopped coming to trade in the city, then poverty and even starvation would not be far away for the men and women of Orvieto.

In fact, bad times were only just round the corner, as the Orvietans were to discover in 1346 and 1347. The war between Benedetto and the Monaldeschi grew more serious. Benedetto's armies were all over the contado, burning houses and trampling the cornfields and vineyards. The prospects for the harvest were anyway poor. It had rained almost without stopping from July to November 1345. Much of the grain had gone rotten, including the seed corn for sowing in the fields the following year. The Orvietans began to feel the pinch in May 1346, and to encourage the local farmers to supply the city, they said that they need not pay the usual tax on all the corn they brought into the city. The council of forty ordered all citizens to tell the captain of the people what stock of corn they had left. At the beginning of July 1346 it was recorded: 'It is clear that corn is getting dearer every day and the harvest is bad.'

The council decided that they had to import corn from outside the contado but corn was short everywhere and they had to pay the high price of 1300 *florins*. To pay for this they made the richer citizens pay a special tax. But this was only a stop-gap and things got worse. In August there were floods in the contado, the war continued, the harvest, as expected, was bad. By the beginning of the next year, 1347, things were getting really bad, though not so disastrous as at Florence where 4,000 people are said to have died of starvation. All the same, prices were going up all round and famine was close. On 31 March 1347 the council freed all the prisoners from gaol, 'for if they remain they will die of hunger'. The dangers of war, the high prices and shortages came to the ears of the travelling merchants. In November 1346 all taxes and tolls had been lifted on travellers beyond the river Tiber who passed through the city or contado but even so merchants were not keen to come to the city. Inside the city the people began to show signs of strain. The poor, on the edge of starva-
40 tion, began to hate the rich: the rich began to fear the poor.

It was fear more than any other reason that made the sixty richest men of the city part with another 1200 florins to buy more corn for the poor.

By the summer of 1347 the war between the local soldiers of Mondaleschi and the papal states had ended and the worst of the famine was over, but merchants were still not keen to come to Orvieto. The council continued to pass laws intended to encourage outsiders to trade and settle in the town. Those who did come would have been depressed by the change which had come over the city. The emergency laws passed in the previous years were still in force. Funerals, usually the occasion for great processions and splendour, were ordered to be conducted simply and cheaply. This is how someone who lived there described the city at this time:

> The houses of the sons of Ernaldo Monaldeschi, the sons of Bernado Monaldeschi have been destroyed by the sons of Bonconte. In the same way Matteo Orsini and the sons of Bonconte have burnt the houses of Guido de Simone in the quarter of S. Giovanni. In the same way Benedetto de Bonconte has burnt numerous villas in the val de Chiana...the castle of Petrorio...houses at Alfina, Sugano and Vallochi. In the same way Corrado di Ermanno destroyed the walls of Ficulle which the people of Parrano have burnt...destroyed the castle of Paterno.

And so the list goes on. War and famine had brought misery, homelessness, debts, disease and destruction to the people of Orvieto. At the end of 1347 many must have breathed a sigh of relief that the bad times were over, hoping and expecting that 1348 would bring a return to peace and prosperity. But almost at that very moment something far worse was on its slow but steady march towards the battered, battle-scarred town.

You can see from the map on page 42 how the Black Death arrived by sea at Genoa at the end of 1347 and spread across Tuscany and Umbria in the early months of 1348. By February it had reached Lucca and news of its approach would certainly have reached Orvieto. What did the council do? Nothing! 41

The people of Orvieto, exhausted and depressed by two [ ] of war and famine, had no fight left in them. Not on [ ] they fail to take the simplest precautions against the [ ] of the plague, but they had lost all interest in doing anything for themselves. In April 1348, after many years, even centuries, fighting to keep their independence, they feebly gave up their liberty and agreed to come under the rule of the city of Perugia, one of their enemies in the recent war with the papal states. In return for their lost liberty, Perugia would pay them a loan of money to pay off the city's debts which had mounted up during the last two years.

The spread of the plague in northern Italy during 1348

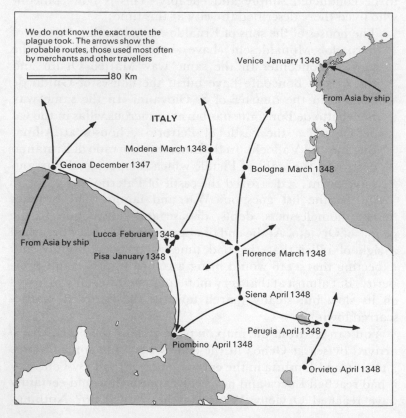

We do not know the exact route the plague took. The arrows show the probable routes, those used most often by merchants and other travellers

⊢————————⊣80 Km

ITALY

Venice January 1348

From Asia by ship

Genoa December 1347

Modena March 1348

Bologna March 1348

Lucca February 1348

Pisa January 1348

Florence March 1348

From Asia by ship

Siena April 1348

Perugia April 1348

Piombino April 1348

Orvieto April 1348

Just as they were drawing up this treaty of surrender, the plague reached Perugia. When Perugia's ambassador arrived in Orvieto on 20 April to make the final arrangements, he brought with him not only the promise of money but almost certainly the plague as well. At the end of the month the first Orvietans began to die. The city was now to suffer its third and worst year of agony. From the beginning of May to the end of August the Black Death raged through the city bringing the pain, the suffering, the spread of disease and death from house to house. The only difference between the behaviour of the plague in villages and towns was that in the towns more people died. In the village of Eyam the parson took certain emergency measures during the plague. Before reading on, pause a moment to consider what steps you think the city council should have taken during the plague months. Remember that up till April nothing had been done. Would there perhaps have been emergency meetings of the council, special laws passed?

You might think so, but what we find is very different. The larger council of forty did not meet at all between May and September. The smaller council, 'the seven', did meet and so did a new emergency council, 'the twelve', chosen by 'the seven' to sit with them. What did they discuss and decide during the plague months? Almost nothing of any importance! Here is a city which has just signed away its independence, a city where people are beginning to die daily by the hundred, yet the council does nothing. Two whole months pass, then on 5 July for the first time the plague is mentioned in the records as 'at present loosing its fearful arrows in all directions'. So what does the council decide? It lays down that because of the shortage of candle-wax resulting from so many funerals, the weight of wax candles for future funerals shall be limited to ten pounds for the nobles, four pounds for the people! Faced with this terrible crisis, all the council can do is to worry about the dead and about preserving class differences.

After 5 July the council does not meet at all for six weeks except to fill the places of councillors who have died—two of 'the seven' in July and four more in August. Two councillors are absent from even these brief meetings. One is said to be ill, the other has probably fled. In short, for the best part of four months during the greatest crisis in its history, the government of the city came almost to a standstill. People died, fled, looted the shops, burgled the houses, the stench of corpses filled the streets but the council did nothing. It was paralysed by fear and so were the rest of the citizens or they would have soon replaced these cowardly rulers with people who knew what to do. But that was the trouble. Nobody did know what to do. So they just did nothing and waited for the nightmare to end. For four months even those whom the Black Death spared were as good as dead. 'The Great Fear', as some called the plague, had utterly defeated the Orvietans. As one eyewitness wrote: 'Many families were wiped out and many houses remained uninhabited. The survivors remained ill and powerless and in great terror abandoned their houses and their dead.'

You should ask yourself the question why it was that the Orvietans lost their nerve so completely, for we know that other Italian cities, Venice for instance, took quick and sensible action against the plague.

In the spring Orvieto had refused to admit that the Black Death was coming, in the summer it desperately tried to pretend that the plague was not there. Only in the autumn, when the plague had passed on, did it admit what a major disaster it had been. Beginning in August with a feeble attempt to control the sale of meat and wine, the council gradually came back to life. From September it sprang into a frenzy of action and reform. The following are just the highlights of the crowded events and decisions of September to December 1348.

In early September the fines imposed on robbers and destroyers of property were doubled. On 19 September there was a meeting of a 'Special General Council of the Nobles and People of Orvieto'. Well over three hundred people attended. They decided by a majority of 317 to 10 to abolish the council of forty and set up new councils of twenty-four and two hundred alongside 'the seven', who were to be assisted by the 'twelve wise men' (a different group from the previous 'twelve'). No nobles were to be allowed to sit on any of the councils. All these changes amounted to a completely new system of government. A whole series of laws were passed by the new councils to restore order in the city and cóntado. A large number of new *notaries* (a mixture of lawyers and accountants) were appointed to replace those who had died, or, in the case of the treasurer's notary, had just disappeared since his appointment in July. Other new appointments included judges and a new captain of the people from Perugia. A great number of wills were *proved* and difficult cases dealt with. For example it was decided that the property of Vanne di Grasso should be divided between his four grandsons since he and his three sons had died since April. It was ordered that a list of orphans without guardians and pupils without tutors should be drawn up, district by district, and new guardians found without delay. Ruined houses were to be repaired and no future destruction of houses was to take place. New and more doctors were to be advertised for and appointed. Their pay was to be increased from twenty-five to a hundred pounds a year, two hundred if they taught as well as practised medicine. (Obviously the Orvietans had not heard of the proverb about shutting the stable door after the horse has bolted!)

On the 30 September it was recorded:

Because of the unheard of, cruel and murderous plague which has recently died down, artisans, masters, labourers and others have so increased their prices that the Orvietans and every one else are justly complaining that if the situation does not immediately improve, they will not be able to carry on their own business, to the great *detriment* of the public good.

The council ordered that prices were not to be increased more than 25%.

On 14 October it was decided that master Andrea di

A plague doctor's costume designed to keep the doctor from any contact with the sick man. The long nose contained perfumes so that the doctor could not smell the sick man. Even the eye-holes are covered with crystal. This illustration is from a French book on plague dated 1721. It is doubtful whether many doctors would actually have worn such an elaborate costume to protect themselves.

Habit des Medecins, et autres personnes qui visitent les Pestiférés, Il est de marroquin de leuant, le masque a les yeux de cristal, et un long néz rempli de parfums

Salamone who had just arrived in the city 'should be treated and considered as a citizen born and brought up in the city since birth.' Before 1348 strangers who came to live in the city had to pay extra taxes and had no rights as citizens at all. But now all that was changed. On 18 October it was publicly announced:

> Since the city of Orvieto, as a result of its troubles, wars, crises and the murderous plague, finds itself short of people both in the city and in the contado, it is necessary to try to repeople it. Every stranger in good health and of good reputation who comes to settle in the city will benefit from

46

complete exemption and immunity from taxes, *posses* and military campaigns for the next ten years...and will be treated and considered as a citizen of the town.

A special fair was organised for 14 November—the normal September fair had of course not taken place—and special measures were passed to encourage merchants to attend.

What of the Church? Like the city council it had tried during the summer to pretend that nothing unusual was happening. In May the feast of Corpus Christi was held as usual. Building work on the cathedral continued at first without a break. Was this a stupid refusal by the Church to face the facts or did they realise that there was nothing helpful that they could do except try to keep up people's confidence by doing their best to carry on normally? Either way, by August even the Church gave up. Work on the cathedral stopped. The feast of the Assumption, one of the special days in the Church's year, was abandoned.

We do not know for certain what the ordinary person in Orvieto thought of the Church's behaviour during the plague, but we have one important clue. On 22 September, a mere fortnight after the plague had finished, the council imposed a tax on the people of the town. At that moment hardly anyone had much money. The first money collected went to the cathedral building fund which was to receive seventy gold florins, a large sum. Was this paid out of respect to the Church and genuine religious belief, or was it an attempt to buy off God's anger in case he should send another plague? Already the Church was saying that the plague was a judgment of God on the sins of the wicked people of the town. (Some may well have wondered why, if that was true, the dead included the Bishop of Orvieto, struck down in far away Avignon while attending the papal court.) The Church was amongst the first to explain why the plague had come, and to try to turn the Black Death disaster to some use. ·Human beings, after they have had a bad shock, have the nasty habit of looking round for someone to blame. We shall learn more about this in Chapter 6.

47

A church procession at Chantilly in France, praying to God to end the plague, with a monk dying on the way. You can read more about people's attitude to the Church after the Black Death in Chapter 7

5 The Black Death Strikes the Citizens: Florence

The city records of Orvieto give us a good idea of what the rulers did or failed to do during the plague period but we can find out little about how the citizens behaved during those five tragic months. How did Vanne di Grasso and his sons spend the long summer days before they were struck down by the plague? Just what did people do, what were their feelings at a time when normal life suddenly stopped and was replaced by fear, chaos and death? The people who wrote the city's records did not mention such things.

Luckily, one of Italy's great writers, Boccaccio, decided to write a book about what a group of ten wealthy young men and women from Florence did during the Black Death. What they did was to move a few miles out of the city to a deserted country house, or villa, and forget all about the troubles by living comfortably, enjoying each other's company and above all by telling stories. These ten people and the stories that they told were made up by Boccaccio, but at the beginning of the book he gives a description of what Florence was really like during the Black Death. As a writer of stories, not history, he was not particularly interested in precisely what orders the city council made. He was interested in how people felt and what they did. Boccaccio never intended what he wrote as history. It is nevertheless the best description of the plague and its effects that we have for 1348. Because it is so good, nearly all the rest of this chapter will consist of what Boccaccio wrote. Of course he wrote in Italian and in language that is not always easy to understand, so what you will read is a simplified and shortened version of what he actually wrote. 49

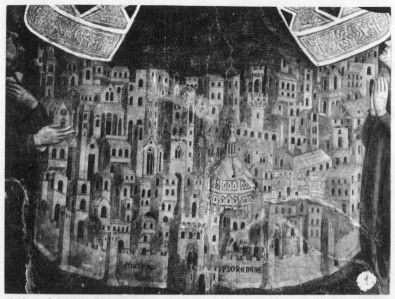

A view of the city of Florence about the time of the Black Death. The fact that the houses were very close together made it easier for the plague to spread

First he describes what the council did as the plague approached: 'Large amounts of refuse were cleared out of the city by specially appointed officials. All ill people were forbidden to enter the city and many instructions were issued to protect people's health, but all in vain.'

Then he goes on to describe the symptoms of the disease, part of which you will find in Chapter 1. Because he was a nobleman (he was Florence's ambassador) he next goes on to describe the behaviour of the upper classes, but these formed only a small part of Florence's large population. To get a general picture it is best to turn first to what Boccaccio has to say later about the way the Black Death struck the ordinary citizens of Florence.

Most were forced by being poor to stay at home. They fell ill by the thousand and having no servants to look after them, they almost all died. Many died in the streets and the death of those who died at home was usually only discovered by neighbours because of the smell of their rotting corpses. Bodies lay all over the place. When someone died, what usually happened was that the neighbours, more for their own health than respect for the dead, took the dead bodies out of the house, with the help of bearers if available, and left them on the front doorstep. The bodies were then carried away in funeral *biers* or just on boards. Often one bier would have two or three bodies in it, husband and wife, brothers and sisters, father and sons, or other close relatives. Very often, as priests were on their way to a funeral, carrying a cross, a queue of three or four biers would form behind them so that they had in the end to cope with not one but seven or eight funerals. There were few bearers and mourners. People had no more respect for the dead than today they would have for a dead animal.

There were so many corpses—more were arriving every hour—that the graveyards were not big enough for each person to have his own grave. When all the graves were full, great trenches were dug and the corpses piled in by

Book illustration from the Middle Ages showing Black Death victims being buried at Tournai in Belgium

the hundred, row upon row, like cargo in a ship, each layer of corpses being covered with a little earth until the trench was full.

Boccaccio could only describe the terrible conditions the ordinary citizens were suffering as an onlooker, but he knew much more about the upper classes. As one of them he knew how they felt as well as how they acted.

Some people believed that by living carefully and eating little, they were less likely to catch the plague, so they formed themselves into groups and lived apart from everyone else. They moved to a comfortable house where there was no one ill and settled down to a peaceful life, eating reasonable amounts of good food and fine wine. They did not speak to outsiders, refused to listen to anything about

An illustration from a printed version of Boccaccio's Decameron, showing a group of wealthy people leading a pleasant life in the countryside while the Black Death rages in Florence

2865 Albany Avenue
West Hartford, CT 06117
4814

the dead or the ill and entertained themselves with music or other amusements which they thought up.

This is very much how Boccaccio's ten imaginary young people behaved. He goes on:

Others thought that the best way to avoid this terrible illness was to drink heavily and enjoy life to the full, to satisfy all one's desires whenever possible and treat the whole thing as an enormous joke. They would go from one pub to another drinking enormous amounts, drinking all day and all night. Or, more often, they would drink in various private houses, but only in those where the conversation was about pleasant, entertaining subjects. Such houses were easy to find, for people behaved as though they were soon to die and did not really care about themselves or their belongings. So most houses became open to all and any passer-by could live there just as though he were the owner. But for all their carefree way of life these people went to great trouble to avoid meeting with those who were ill...

There were many others who found a middle way between these two ways of behaving. Instead of shutting themselves up they moved around normally, holding in their hands a posy of flowers or sweet-smelling herbs, or one of many spices, which they frequently sniffed, for the stink of dead bodies, disease and medicines seemed to fill and pollute the whole air.

Some people, taking what was possibly a safer way out, selfishly decided that the best way to avoid the plague was to run away from it.... thinking of no one but themselves, large numbers of men and women left their city, their homes, their relations, their houses and their belongings and set off for the countryside.

Of course, none of these different ways of behaving, even running away, could save people from catching the plague. What happened then?

Many, having set a [bad] example when they were fit and well, died with almost no one to nurse them. Not only   53

Townspeople fleeing into the country from the plague of 1630

did citizens avoid each other, neglect their neighbours and seldom visit their relations, talking to them only from a safe distance; people were so terrified of the plague that brothers abandoned each other, uncles left nephews, wives even deserted their husbands. Worse still, and almost unheard of, parents refused to nurse and look after their own children, acting as though they were nothing to do with them.

So the vast number of people who fell ill had to depend entirely either on the help of friends—who were few and far between—or on the few greedy servants who remained getting much higher wages than they deserved for the little they did. These servants were rough types and untrained who did little more than hand things when asked to the invalid and stand there as he lay dying. The greed of these servants often cost them their lives. So a great many people died who might have perhaps survived if they had been given more help.

So even the wealth of the nobles could not save them from a painful death. Faced with a calamity, the upper classes soon lost their manners and their neighbourliness. Good christian behaviour disappeared and even family ties were not strong enough to keep people together in this crisis. Ordinary civilised life, as we know it and the Florentines knew it, was replaced by a cruel and selfish 'live and let die' attitude. Boccaccio only writes of how the nobles behaved. As so often in history we do not really know how the ordinary people reacted. How do you think that their behaviour would have compared with that of the nobility? How some people behaved, who were neither ordinary nor noble, you can read about in the next chapter.

6 Reactions to the Black Death: the Flagellants

At Orvieto it was noticeable that very soon after the plague was over, the Church began to say that God had sent it because of people's sinful ways. In Florence during the plague people did some desperate things, deserting their own children and running away. A mixture of despair and a deep sense of sin led several groups to behave in a remarkable way in a feverish attempt to wipe out their sins and stop God's anger.

There always were and still are religious *fanatics* who believe that by *mortifying* the flesh they can drive away the devil and wash away their sins. (A certain saint Simon Stylites lived for thirty years on top of a tall pillar.) But when times are good these fanatics have few followers. When times are bad, when the world seems to be crumbling about people's ears, many turn to the fanatics in the desperate hope that perhaps they can really do something to save the situation. One of the most incredible of these fanatic groups were the flagellants. Flagellants believed that by beating themselves or each other and doing painful things to their bodies they would make up for their sins and have more chance of going to heaven when they died. This is what a flagellant friar in the 1400s did:

He shut himself up in his cell and stripped himself naked ...and took his scourge with the sharp spikes, and beat himself on the body and on the arms and on the legs, till blood poured off him as from a man who has been *cupped*. One of the spikes on the scourge was bent crooked, like a hook, and whatever flesh it caught it tore off. He beat himself so hard that the scourge broke into three bits and the points flew against the wall. He stood there bleeding and gazed at himself. . . . Out of pity for himself he began to weep bitterly. And he knelt down, naked and covered in blood, in the frosty air, and prayed to God to wipe out his sins from before his gentle eyes.

The first time the flagellant movement became popular in Europe was in 1260, an earlier year of crisis, of war and disease. Nearly ninety years later, as the Black Death spread across Europe, came a second great wave of flagellant groups, anything from fifty to five hundred people marching from town to town. At Tournai in modern Belgium, the bewildered abbot recorded on 15 August 1349 the arrival of 200 flagellants from Bruges. During the next week came 400 from Ghent, 300 from Sluis, 400 from Dordrecht, 180 from Liège. On 7 September amid scenes of wild excitement the men of Tournai formed their own band, and 565 men set off for Liège.

Flagellants, bare to the waist, beating each other. Because they are holding a banner and a crucifix as well as whips it is clear that the flagellants thought of what they did as a kind of religious service

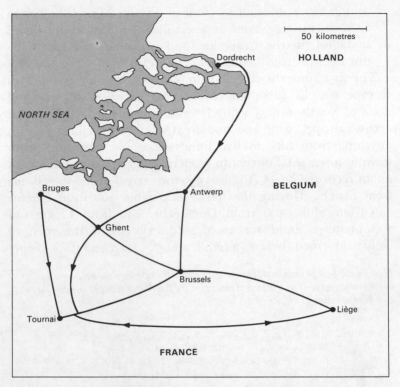

The recorded movements of the flagellants in north-west Europe in 1349. (In 1349 Holland and Belgium were part of the Holy Roman Empire which also included Germany, Switzerland, and parts of Eastern France)

Between 12 September and 23 October about 3,500 flagellants passed through the town.

The leaders of the Church did not quite know what to do about the flagellants. They approved of the idea that people should confess their sins and do *penance* for them but they were embarrassed by the extraordinary scenes that went on in their churches and angry that the flagellants felt able to do without priests, especially in Germany where priests were openly criticised. On the whole the flagellants did little harm. They hurt their own bodies but perhaps as a result did feel better in their minds. They criticised the priests, but then they were far from perfect. Unfortunately, among the more extreme groups, an uglier side of human nature began to show itself. Most flagellants thought that the Black Death was God's punishment on them for their sins, but some of the more unpleasant began to put the blame on other men. In the usual way of bullies, they picked on people who were weak and already unpopular—the Jews. This was not the first or the last time that the Jews would be accused of something that they never did. Smear campaigns started. For instance, Jews were accused of poisoning a town's water supply, and soon more and more people in their fear and hate were taking it out on the Jews. 1348–49 saw the worst *massacre* of Jews in Europe until in the 1940s Hitler set a new grim record of man's brutality.

The worst massacres were in Germany and modern Belgium. In Brussels, as the flagellants approached, every single one of the six hundred Jews in the city was killed by the in-

Jews being burnt in Germany

People accused of spreading the plague being tortured in Milan in 1630

habitants. In Mainz, which had the largest Jewish community in Germany, a massacre of the Jews suddenly started in the middle of a flagellant meeting and the whole community was wiped out. Tragically, these mass murderers believed that they were doing what God wanted them to do. Those rulers who tried to protect the Jews were either ignored or themselves attacked. By 1351 there were hardly any Jews left in Europe.

There were other *scapegoats* as well as the Jews, but always the weak and defenceless: old ladies living alone and suspected of being witches: village idiots: even dogs. But the rats, the real spreaders of the plague went unharmed.

If the bloody bodies of the flagellants make you feel sick and the Jew-killers make you angry, you must remember that they were desperate men, acting almost without thinking, caught up in a great crowd, doing what they did in the heat of the moment. Others behaved less violently but with a cold selfishness. There were many in authority who should have tried to lead and to help but in fact only thought of their own skins. Sadly, many churchmen behaved like this. In England William of Dene, a monk at Rochester wrote:

During the whole of that winter and the following spring [1348/9] the Bishop of Rochester, aged and infirm, remained at Trottiscliffe [his country manor]. In the monastery of Rochester supplies ran short and the monks had great difficulty in getting enough to eat, so much so that they were forced either to grind their own bread or go without. The prior however ate everything of the best.

It is easy to sympathise with the tired old bishop. It was all too much for him. No one except themselves felt sorry for the monks having to make their own bread, but how everyone must have hated the prior! Another monk, at Canterbury, wrote: 'The parish churches remained altogether unserved, and parsons turned away from the care of *benefices* for fear of death.'

There is no doubt that many clergy died performing their duties to the last. It is equally certain that many others just ran away.

There are always some people who manage to turn any event, however unpleasant, to their own profit. Typical of these were those who sold medicines and magic charms against the plague. Here are three examples:

The best pills generally under heaven—take the best yellow *aloes,* two ounces, *myrrh* and *saffron,* of each one ounce; beat them together in a *mortar* a good while. Put in a little sweet wine, then roll it up and of this make five pills... Take one a day next (to) your heart, a *scruple* or more, and it will *expulse* the pestilence that day.

A most excellent drink against the plague—take three *gills* of the best *Malmsey;* boil it till one pint be boiled away; put thereto long pepper, ginger and nutmegs beaten ...let all these boil together. Put in one ounce of *mithridatum* and two ounces of *treacle Venice* and a quarter pint of *aqua vitae.* Take morning and evening one spoonful. There never was man, woman or child that this drink deceived.

Take a live frog, and lay the belly of it next the plague

61

Medicines being weighed and mixed in a apothecary's (chemist's) shop. Although many medicines in the Middle Ages were definitely useless, it is wrong to believe that they all did no good just because they seem odd to us

sore; if the patient will escape, the frog will burst in a quarter of an hour; then lay on another; and this you do till more do burst, for they draw forth the *venom*. If none of the frogs do burst, the party [person] will not escape. This hath been frequently tried. Some say a dried toad will do it better.

Perhaps you want to laugh at people that could be silly enough to believe that any of these medicines or charms would work, but don't forget that tourist shops today are full 'lucky pixies', St Christophers and so on and that many well-known people who lead dangerous lives like some racing drivers and mountaineers always wear lucky charms. You may think that people who are *superstitious* are stupid, but they are not bad. But what about those who sold these medicines knowing them to be useless? Could they defend themselves from the charge that they deserved contempt for making money by false pretences out of other people's misfortunes?

7   After the Black Death

Chapter 3 describes what happened to two manors after the Black Death. Things turned out rather differently in each. In one, houses lay empty and fields uncultivated for quite a long time. In the other, life quickly returned to something like normal. At Witney the lord decided to make big changes in his farming methods, replacing corn with sheep and leasing the home farm out to a tenant. At Brightwell, the changes were less important.

Chapter 4 describes Orvieto's terrible plight during and immediately after the plague. In fact Orvieto never recovered its former prosperity and independence. It came under the rule of the popes and when two rival popes were chosen, it again became a battleground. In the siege of 1380 three thousand people were killed. By 1400 there were less than half the number of people in the town than there had been a hundred years before. Certainly the Black Death had a lot to do with this collapse but it would probably be wrong to blame everything on it. What does seem certain is that a combination of a fierce war, near famine and the Black Death so shocked the Orvietans that they lost the will to win back their former prosperity and independence.

In Florence an even greater proportion of the people died than in Orvieto and during the Black Death everyone felt just as unable to do anything about it, as described in Chapter 5. Yet by 1400 Florence was more powerful and prosperous than ever before. In the town records of Orvieto the Black Death is constantly used as an excuse for the city's decline from its former glory. The Florentines soon put the Black

Florence in 1580. Between 1400 and 1500 Florence became probably the most important city in Italy, a centre of trade, banking and the arts. Like Orvieto earlier, it lost some of its power and wealth after 1500 because it was involved in a long series of wars

Death out of their minds and got on with rebuilding their fortunes to new heights.

From all this you can see that people who ask the question—what were the results of the Black Death?—cannot be given a simple, short answer. Some places suffered much more than others, and even when two places suffered about the same amount at the time, the final results were different. There is a further difficulty. It is very tempting for historians, as it was for the city councillors of Orvieto, to believe that the Black Death was the cause of anything unpleasant that happened after it. This is by no means always true even of the decline in the number of people. We know, as mentioned in Chapter 3, that in many parts of Europe the population was already going down before 1348. We also know that in Florence after the Black Death, and at Eyam after the 1666 plague, the population quickly grew back to its former size, yet the population of England as a whole took about three hundred years to get back to its 1347 figure! Fourteenth-century England behaved differently from seventeenth-century

England and fourteenth-century Florence yet all suffered from the same plague. Can one really say then that it was the Black Death's fault that the population of England went down and stayed down?

Despite all these differences, a historian must try to paint a general picture of the results of the Black Death in Europe. But remember when you read descriptions of this kind, whether in this book or any other, that in many parts of Europe what actually happened may well have been the exact opposite of what is described.

Perhaps the truest thing that one can say about the Black Death is that it acted as a *catalyst*. It had the result of enormously speeding up things that were beginning to happen already. For instance, on manors where tenants were beginning to pay money to their lord rather than work for him in return for their land, this change to money rents was speeded up. Towns like Orvieto in Italy and Norwich in England, which had been prosperous but before 1348 were already beginning to go down hill slowly, now slid down much faster into poverty.

It is also generally true that wages went up all over Europe despite the efforts of rulers to pass laws to prevent this. For example, the *Statute* of Labourers of 1351 in England fixed a maximum legal wage in order to keep prices down and prevent labourers from leaving their masters for better-paid work somewhere else. Just as the laws of modern governments have failed to keep wages and prices down, so the Statute of Labourers was in the long run a failure, but for a few years it was certainly as successful as any modern prices and incomes policy. Everyone thought it was a good idea for others, but were quite ready to break the law themselves. Landlords illegally paid more than the maximum wage to bribe labourers away from their neighbours' estates. Peasant labourers, realising that they were now in a good position to bargain, also willingly broke the law and became angry with the lords and government who tried to prevent them doing well for themselves.

It is not such a big jump from groups of angry peasants here and there to the idea of a full-scale peasant revolt against landlords and governments. It is certainly true that there are more than the usual number of peasants' revolts in Europe after 1350 than before. The most famous are the Jacquerie in France in 1358 and the Peasants Revolt in England in 1381. Here we have another example of the temptation to believe that the Black Death caused the Peasants' revolts because they broke out not long after 1348. There are, however, many other convincing reasons for the revolts. The French peasants had suffered badly from the war which the English had been fighting across their fields for the last twenty years, a war in which the French army had just been soundly beaten. Rather like the supporters of a modern soccer club, the French peasants went mad.

The English peasants had just had to suffer a series of very heavy and most unfair taxes. It would be quite easy to 'prove' that the Black Death had nothing to do with the peasants revolts. Actually, the causes of events are very seldom simple or straight-forward, and although opinions differ on how much the Black Death had to do with the revolts, all historians believe it did play some part. What it did was to change the peasants' way of looking at life, to shake them out of their old ways, to start them thinking. Having found out how nice it was to be a little richer, they began to realise how much they had been missing all these years. A few of the most intelligent, 'the hedgerow priests' as they were often called, began to put ideas into their minds, to fill their heads with slogans that they could easily understand. 'When Adam *delved* and Eve *span,* who was then the gentleman?' preached John Ball, hedgerow priest and one of the leaders of the Peasants Revolt. What he meant by this was that in the beginning everyone was equal, so now lords and gentlemen should divide their riches equally with the peasants.

Another hedgerow priest was William Langland, who was also a very fine poet. About 1370 he wrote a book in verse called 'Piers the Ploughman'. This is a religious book in which the narrator, Will, searches for salvation helped by visions of Piers the Ploughman. In the stories Langland describes all

John Ball preaching. His listeners, if they are supposed to be peasants, are too well dressed and armoured!

the people of his day, from the puffed up courtier to the rogues and beggars. In one story Piers asks a group of pilgrims to help him sow his fields before he leads them on a pilgrimage. At first they agree but then things start to go wrong.

Then Waster would not work any more but set out as a tramp, and beggars refused the bread that had beans in it, demanding milk loaves and fine wheaten bread, and they would not drink cheap beer at any price but only the best brown ale that is sold in the towns. And the day-labourers who have no land to live on but their shovels would not *deign* to eat yesterday's vegetables. And *draught ale* was not good enough for them, nor a hunk of bacon, but they must have fresh meat or fish, fried or baked or hot from the oven at that, lest they catch a chill on their stomachs. And so it is nowadays—the labourer is angry unless he gets high wages and curses the day he was ever 67 born a workman....He blames God and curses the king and his council for making statutes on purpose to plague the workmen.

Though Langland does not actually say that the Black Death is the reason why beggars and labourers have got above themselves, when he mentions 'statutes to plague the workmen' he is almost certainly thinking of the Statute of Labourers. Unlike John Ball, William Langland did not preach rebellion but he criticised the upper classes just as much as the day-labourers. Most of all however he criticised the Church:

I saw pilgrims and palmers [professional pilgrimage goers] banding together to visit the shrines at Rome and Compostella [a famous pilgrim centre in Spain] and took leave to tell fibs about it for the rest of their lives....Troops of hermits with their hooked *staves* were on their way to Walsingham [a famous English pilgrim centre] with their wenches [mistresses] following after. These great long *lubbers* who hated work were got up in clerical gowns to distinguish them from laymen and paraded as hermits for the sake of an easy life. I saw the Friars there too, preaching to the people for what they could get. In their greed for fine clothes they interpreted the scriptures to suit themselves and their *patrons*. There was also the *Pardoner*...he produced a document which claimed to have the power *to absolve* all the people from broken fasts and vows of every kind. The ignorant folk believed him and were delighted. They came up and knelt to kiss his documents while he...raked in their rings and jewellery with his roll of parchment....Then I heard parish priests complaining to the Bishop that since the Plague their parishes were too poor to live in, so they asked permission to live in London where they could traffic in masses [earn money by holding services for rich people] and chime their voices to the sweet jingling of silver....Bishops, Doctors of Divinity and the other great divines [important church-men], I saw them all living in London. Some took posts at court counting the king's money...others went into

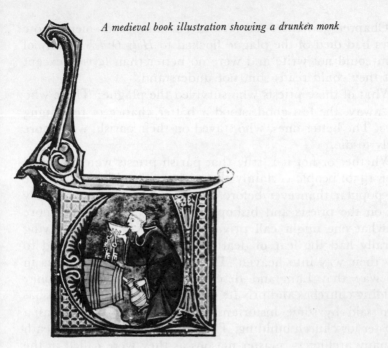

A *medieval book illustration showing a drunken monk*

the service of lords and ladies, sitting like stewards managing household affairs....I fear there are many whom Christ will curse for ever.

As Langland was a priest himself, he probably did not exaggerate the poor state the Church was in. Of course there always had been lazy priests and worldly bishops, but it does seem that the Church after 1350 was in a worse condition than before. Again the question crops up—was the Black Death the cause, or was the Church going down hill anyway? Two things suggest that the Black Death did play a part. Chapter 8 tells how over most of England nearly half the parish priests had died and had to be replaced inside two years. Many of the replacements must have been chosen in a hurry. The bishop, safely shut away in his country house, might be less careful than usual to appoint a good, well trained priest, even if such a man could be found. Henry Knighton, a monk at Leicester whose description of the plague appears in Chapter 3, wrote: 'A very large number of men whose wives had died of the plague flocked to *Holy Orders*. Many of them could not write and were no better than *laymen,* except that they could read—but not understand.'

What of those priests who survived the plague? Those who ran away, the less good, stood a better chance of remaining alive. The better ones, who stayed on their parish, were more likely to die.

Whether or not it is true that parish priests were less good after 1350, people certainly thought so. The Church became less popular than ever before. Ordinary people came to rely less on the priests and bishops for their salvation and more on what one might call private insurance schemes. Having literally had the fear of death put into them, they tried to buy their way into heaven. The poor used the pardoners in the way that Langland describes. The rich spent money building churches and private chapels, called chantries. It has been said by some historians that the Black Death was a disaster for church building. This is not really true. The death of many architects, master-masons as they were called in the Middle Ages, probably reduced the standard of workmanship, and temporary shortage of money and labour caused some of the grander building plans to be abandoned. But the number of churches built and the additions made to existing ones increased. Winchester cathedral is a good example.

The Black Death arrived at Winchester just as Bishop Edington was about to rebuild the west end of the cathedral. As the old west end had already been knocked down, the bishop had to change his original grand plans and put up a 'temporary' front—which still stands today! Edington was unable to afford to do any more building. If you study the graphs of the profits from two of his manors given in Chapter 3 (pages 27 and 29) you will see why. You will also see why his successor, William of Wykeham, was not only rich enough to build a new college at Oxford University (still called New College) and a 'school for poor scholars' in Winchester itself but also to rebuild the nave of the cathedral completely. By a

The north transept of Winchester cathedral built in the Norman style about 1100 AD. Until William of Wykeham's rebuilding, the whole cathedral was built in this style

The nave of Winchester cathedral after being changed by William of Wykeham. Compare this with the transept stroke of genius he turned it into a grand church in the latest 'Perpendicular' style without knocking anything down. William Wynford, architect of all these new building projects was as brilliant as any architect before the Black Death, and Henry Yevele who built the nave at Canterbury cathedral was as good. Do not believe anyone or any book that tells you that the Perpendicular style was another thing caused by the Black Death, a cheap and easy style for an age of poverty. William Ramsey, the architect who first built in the new style, died of the plague in 1349, and if you look at the size and magnificence of a church like Beverley minster in Yorkshire, you will see that it cannot have been cheap to put up.

So far in this chapter we have considered the effects or possible effects of the Black Death on cities, manors, the size of the population, on wages and prices, peasants and labourers, the Church and church architecture. Quite a long list, but of course nothing like a complete one. Almost everyone, every activity, was or could have been affected by the Black Death. For instance, scholars complained that so many Latin teachers died of the plague that students could no longer write or speak the language properly. To try to complete the list would take a long time and would become boring. You might like to imagine for yourselves other things in life which the Black Death affected.

If you have read this chapter carefully, you may have noticed that one thing keeps re-appearing. The Black Death changed the way people thought and felt. The Orvietans lost the will to struggle, peasants became discontented, people generally became *cynical* about the Church. The really important thing about the Black Death is that it changed people's attitude to life. They became more pessimistic, more cynical, more inclined to be selfish. Of course not everyone was an *optimist* before 1348 and a *pessimist* after 1350, but there would have been very few people whose view of life became rosier after the Black Death, even if in some ways they were better off. This general gloom and dissatisfaction lasted not just for a year or two, or for ten years, but for a century or more.

A book illustration showing 'the three living and the three dead', suggesting that the three young women would soon be corpses

Not only those who lived through the Black Death but their sons, and their grandchildren, took a grimmer view of life. The reasons for this long-lasting mood of *depression* in Europe is not as simple as you might think. Certainly the Black Death was very unpleasant and did a lot of damage; certainly the plague kept on coming back after 1348. Yet plague was only one among very many unpleasant and fatal diseases which men and women of the time had to suffer. They had also suffered, long before 1348, from frequent wars, bad harvests, droughts and floods, leading to famine. Such things were quite usual, yet people remained reasonably happy and confident. Just as in wartime or a crisis period people often become friendlier, more ready to help each other, even happier, so medieval men learned to help each other out in the bad times. But the Plague was different. It was disgusting, it was mysterious, it was all-powerful. For those who survived the Black Death the experience was so dreadful that the memory of it continued to haunt them. They passed their fears on to their children and this fear of the plague was in a way worse than the plague itself. What was the good of making plans and working hard to save money when the day after tomorrow you might be dead? This is what many people now felt— or so we believe. It is difficult to be certain because the plague caused such a deep feeling of dread that people were afraid to talk or write about it, much as today many people will not talk about cancer, another painful disease that strikes from nowhere.

People suffering from such a deep fear behave in different ways. In much the same way as those whom Boccaccio described in Florence (see Chapter 5), many decided to 'eat drink and be merry, for tomorrow we die'. Only the nobles could usually afford to do this. We find them in many courts living half their life in a round of *banquets*, festivals and entertainments, and listening to stories of the 'good old days' of long ago.

'The dance of death', a woodcut made in 1493. This was a very common subject for drawings and paintings at this time

Often they dressed themselves up as people of legend and acted out their adventures, or fought mock wars according to rules long out of date. This was the time when the stories of King Arthur and his knights of the Round Table, and other such stories, became very popular. The stories were re-written and added to, and illustrated in beautifully written books with scenes from the adventures. Nowhere was more money spent on creating a make-believe world of love and adventure than in the court of the Dukes of Burgundy in France.

The nobles tried to shut out the grim reality by inventing an imaginary world but the artists and writers employed by the Duke of Burgundy and other wealthy nobles could not always manage to forget their inner fears. Many of the pictures and the writings of this period have to do with death and with hell, with torture, witchcraft and damnation. Some of the most gruesome and gloomy pictures, such as those by Hieronymous Bosch, were painted at this time and evil books were written like the 'Malleus Mallificorum', a brutal handbook for detecting and punishing supposed witches.

Those who had no taste or no money for make-believe often became very keen on religion. Despairing of this life, they tried to prepare themselves for the next. They had little faith left in ordinary churchmen, bishops and priests; still less in quarrelsome monks and greedy friars. So they tried to find their own way to God and became *mystics*, spending long hours in thought and contemplation, inventing what amounted almost to a private religion. Others joined up with people like themselves to form new religious groups. Two of the greatest mystics, St Thomas à Kempis and St Teresa belong to this time, as does a very successful religious group called the Brethren of the Common Life.

There were some who were dissatisfied both with their religious and with their lay leaders and became rebels against the church and the king. In England, around 1400, many became Lollards, *heretics* who wanted great changes in the Church and a better deal for the peasants from their lords. In Bohemia (modern Czechoslovakia) the people were ruled by Germans whom they hated as foreigners. There the rebels, the Hussites, became freedom-fighting patriots as well as heretics.

Part of a large picture of hell by Bosch painted in the later Middle Ages. This picture is full of weird and horrid details. It is easy to believe that the painter had a sick imagination

But most of the people of Europe showed their dissatisfaction with life and fear of the future quite simply. They brought fewer children into the world. It has often been shown that when people are confident about the future they have large families. When the future looks grim or uncertain families are smaller. This fact answers a question asked earlier: was it the plague which caused the population to go down and stay down? The answer we can now see is: not the plague itself (the number it killed could have been quickly replaced) but the fear of the plague made people unwilling to bring children into the world. There were exceptions of course, like Florence, but in England and Europe as a whole, gloom and uncertainty kept the population down.

It would be quite wrong to leave you with the idea that the coming of the Black Death and the fear that followed it were the only things that brought about this change of mood in Europe. There were longer and more destructive wars than earlier and for various other reasons life became more unpleasant between 1350 and 1450 than it had been during the two hundred years before the Black Death. But it was the Black Death more than any other single thing which made the last century of what we call the Middle Ages, despite the many beautiful churches, the prosperous Italian and south German towns, despite the flowering of a great new time of painting, architecture, *sculpture* and literature in Italy, a dark age, an age of deep fear. This flowering of the arts in Italy is called the *Renaissance* and is thought by many to be the start of a new, confident age, of modern times. Yet one of the subjects most often painted by Renaissance artists is the 'Martyrdom of St Sebastian', pictures of a man shot through with many arrows, a way for the artist to express pain, suffering and fear. It is not surprising that St Sebastian was the patron saint of those who caught the plague, the saint to whom they prayed to save their lives.

Nevertheless, round about 1500, the mood of Europe did gradually change for the better, well before the plague disappeared. Plague only began to leave Europe in the later

*Dürer's version of
'the martyrdom of
St. Sebastian'*

1600s but the deep fear of it was gradually conquered. When bad plagues hit London in 1603 and 1665, people were no longer too frightened to write about it. Remedies for the plague, plays, and sermons about it poured from the printing presses. Tens of thousands died in London but its population went on rising fast. Plague was still a killer but it was no longer deeply frightening. Europe had at last learnt to live with the plague without fear.

8 How Many People Died?

The Black Death made such an impression on the people of the day that they wrote about it much more than about the more ordinary things in their lives. We call what the people of the day wrote our sources for history but it would take you too long to read about all the sources from which it is possible for historians today to discover about the plague. Some of the sources, however, and some of the problems of discovering the truth from them can be illustrated by considering just one question: how many people died of the Black Death? The honest answer to this question is 'we don't know', but we can make a sensible guess by studying the surviving records. As these have survived better in England than anywhere else we will consider how many died in England rather than in the whole of Europe.

It might seem obvious that the difference between the number of people living in England in 1347 and the number living in 1350 would give us the number who died of the Black Death. But that would be to forget that, even during the plague, some people died of old age and other diseases or accidents. Anyway we do not know exactly how many people were living in England in 1347 and 1350. The nearest we can get is that just before the Black Death the population of England was about four million and that thirty years later it had fallen to about two and a half million. Even though there were other less serious outbreaks of plague between 1348 and 1377, this tremendous drop in numbers does suggest that a very large number of people died of the Black Death.

People who lived at the time tried to estimate how many

people had died in their town. Boccaccio, whose description of the Black Death appears in Chapters 1 and 5, said that at Florence 100,000 people died in 1348. This is about 10,000 more than the total number of people living in the town at the time! Making accurate estimates is not easy—try to estimate the size of your town or village—but medieval men were particularly weak at arithmetic. They were especially vague about big numbers. They did not really mean literally the big round numbers they wrote down any more than you do when you tell your friend: 'I have got thousands of marbles at home.' So, for the historian, estimates by people at the time of how many died are generally not much use and anyway tell us nothing about how many people died in England as a whole.

Fortunately there are other kinds of documents made at the time which suffer less from guesswork and poor arithmetic. When a man dies, especially if he is someone quite rich or important, the fact that he has died will be recorded in a number of places. For one thing, he will make a will and before this will can be proved, that is, before his heirs get their share of his goods or money, someone has to count up how much money he has and put a value on his goods. This was done in the Middle Ages by holding an 'Inquisitio Post Mortem' (literally an enquiry after death). Many of these inquisitions have survived and by counting up the number made in 1348 and 1349 and comparing it with the number made in say 1340 and 1341 we can get an idea of how many more people died during the Black Death. Some actual wills have survived too and these can be counted in the same way.

In the Middle Ages many people leased land from the lord of the manor. When they died the lord had to find a new tenant who would then pay the lord a sum of money to take over the land (see Chapter 3). This money was paid in at the manor court and the sum paid was written down in the manorial court roll. Many of these court rolls survive so it is possible to find out how many more new tenants than usual took over land in the years immediately after 1348. As you saw in Chapter 3, at Witney, in some manors the increase in new tenants is very great and in some court rolls it is recorded that no new tenants could be found to take the place of those who had died. Now if this had happened before 1348 it would have been very surprising, for we know that there was always a long waiting list of people without land hoping to get some (rather like waiting to get a council house these days.) So it looks as though on those manors in which lands lay empty after 1348 the number of people who died must have been very high indeed. Confusingly, in some manors, as at Brightwell (see Chapter 3), few tenants died and those that did were quickly replaced so that we know for certain that the plague struck unevenly. But it is very difficult to work out how many people died altogether. Some parts of England were not organised into manors and many manor court rolls have been lost over the years so there still has to be a lot of guesswork. It is perhaps not so surprising that some expert historians believe that over England as a whole only two out of ten died while others believe it was nearer six out of ten!

One kind of record survives better than any other from the Middle Ages. As you may know, churchmen were far better educated than laymen. Indeed, until near the end of the Middle Ages very few laymen could write at all. So it is no coincidence that the records of the churches were the best kept and the best preserved. Now when a parish priest died, it was up to the local bishop to make sure a replacement was found as soon as possible. As a bishop would have several hundred parishes in the diocese under his control he needed a record of who was in charge of each parish. When a new priest was instituted, that is, took over a parish, his name was entered in the bishop's record. These records of the institution of new priests have survived for most of England for the period of the Black Death. If we look at the numbers of new clergy instituted in 1348 and 1349 county by county or *diocese* by diocese, the proportion of new priests taking over parishes works out very much the same in every area. We can therefore be fairly certain that between four and five out of every ten parish priests died in England during the Black Death. But what does this tell us about the rest of the people of England? Here the experts start arguing again. Were the parish priests more likely to die than others because they attended the bedsides of the dying or were they less likely to die because they lived in better houses—or maybe equally likely to die? Every expert has his own view on this but there is very little evidence to support their views one way or the other.

Evidence is as important to the historian as it is to the lawyer or the detective. Like a good detective, a good historian does not only look in the obvious places for his evidence and when he is puzzled he often turns to experts in other subjects to help him. The police inspector turns to the doctor to know whether the blood on the accused's shirt matches the blood of the murdered victim. The historian interested in plague also turns to the medical experts. The latest professor of medicine to write about the Black Death has shocked the historians by stating very firmly that from what we know about plague as a disease it is impossible that more than two out of ten people in England died of the Black Death and even two out of ten is probably too many. Of course experts can be wrong and others are busy looking for the flaw in the professor's case and so the argument goes on.

It may seem to you that if experts disagree so widely in their views on how many people died then it is hardly worth while for ordinary people like us to worry about it. It obviously does make a difference whether six out of ten or only two out of ten died of the Black Death but not as much difference as you might expect. If you think about it, the fact that in England as a whole a certain number of people died does not really mean very much. It is what happens in a particular town or village that is important. All the experts agree that in some villages and in many towns over half the population died. For the people in those places, alive or dead, the Black Death was a catastrophe and it is certain that there were enough of those places for the Black Death to have been a nation-wide disaster even if some areas got off much more lightly.

And what of the places where only two out of ten died? Think back to your class of thirty. Think of the effect on you and your friends if six of your classmates were to die of a foul disease during the next two terms. There are a number of ways you might react—run away, get very frightened, or depressed, and so on—but probably your feelings would not be very different from those in a class in a neighbouring school where eighteen out of thirty died.

We should beware of getting too worked up about exact numbers in history. It is the duty of the experts to make the most accurate estimate they can from the evidence they have. What the rest of us need to think about is what a certainly very large number of sudden deaths meant to people, how they felt and what they did about it. All the same it is as well for us to be aware of the many things—not just the number of people who died—that we and the experts do not know for certain about the Black Death.

9 How and Why the Black Death Happened

The most important things about the Black Death are that it happened and that it had important effects on the way people lived and thought. All the same, in history as in other subjects we cannot help wondering why things happened. Occasionally, discovering why things happened can help prevent them from happening again. Before anyone could find out why plague arrived in Europe in 1348 they had to understand exactly what plague was and how it spread. This was not possible until medical science had become much more advanced than it was in the Middle Ages. It was only about eighty years ago that plague was properly understood by doctors. Even today there are disagreements between experts about how people catch the plague because the story is a complicated one. What follows is a simplified version of what most doctors now believe about plague.

The disease itself takes the form of a *bacillus* (plural, bacilli) or bacterium, an older word for the same thing. Bacilli are so small that they are only visible under a microscope and would have been quite invisible to medieval man. The bacilli normally lived in and infected a particular kind of flea. This flea in turn normally lived on a rat, the black rat, sometimes called the house or ship rat. At the time when the Black Death arrived in Europe black rats were common in men's houses, living in the roof thatch or even in the straw that most people used for beds. A man could be infected by plague when he was bitten by an infected flea. Now, though it may seem strange, fleas are usually fussy about what they eat. A rat flea does not like to bite a human if there is a rat about. When

A rat flea (many times larger than life-size!)

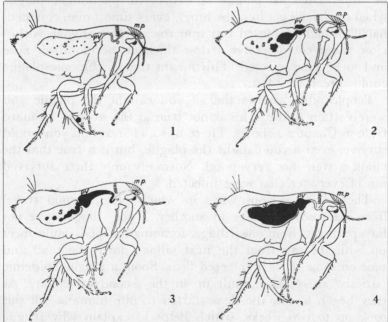

A plague infected rat flea. The dark spots in the first picture are the plague bacilli which multiply rapidly to block the flea's stomach as is shown happening in the other pictures

however a rat flea was infected with the plague the entrance to its stomach became completely blocked with bacilli and it became madly hungry. Quite possibly at this moment the rat it had been living on died of plague and the ravenous flea left it to bite the first flesh it could find, most probably a human being, though dogs, cats and other animals were also infected. When a flea bites, it makes a tiny puncture in the skin, and sucks blood. When an infected flea bit, the blood it swallowed met the bacilli at the entrance of the stomach and because it could not enter the stomach was spat out again. The blood infected with bacilli remained under the man's skin. After that it was probably only a matter of time before that person fell ill. Ordinary human fleas can carry the plague, so if one person caught an infected flea from his neighbour, he could catch the plague as well. With pneumonic plague when the bacilli got into the lungs, every time a man coughed, bacilli would be hurled out into the air and anyone within close range could receive a dose through the mouth or nose and so become infected. This meant that pneumonic plague could spread very fast.

People often assume that if you caught the plague you were certain to die. This is not true as the story of Leonard Gale in Chapter 2 shows. There was a chance that you would survive, even if you caught the plague, but it is true that the chances were not very good. Normally only three survived out of every ten that were infected.

There were various ways in which plague could travel from one town or village to another. If the villages were not far apart, rats from one village, foraging for food, could meet up with the rats from the next village down the road and pass on some of their infected fleas. Soon, a plague epidemic (strictly, an *epizootic*) built up in the second rat colony. As they began to die, the fleas started to bite humans. All this took up to two weeks, which helps to explain why plague often spread quite slowly. It also explains how villagers who cut themselves off completely from all human contact were 86 still not safe from the plague.

The Black Rat

Alternatively, a traveller, infected but not yet obviously ill, could introduce the disease to the local rats or people. He would sicken and die. Then, after an ominous pause of a week or so, the epidemic would begin. It was also possible for an infected flea, if kept warm, to remain alive for several days, perhaps weeks, without a living body to feed on. Bales of wool, or parcels of clothes often acted as the fatal carrier, for wool, medieval Europe's major industry, was for ever on the move all over Europe.

So in 1348 the Black Death arrived from Asia by sea, carried by ships' rats or infected sailors. It struck the ports and from them, carried either slowly by rats or a little more quickly by travellers or cargoes of wool, fanned out in all directions across Europe, spreading chiefly along the well-known trade routes.

All this explains how the plague spread but it does not explain why it arrived in 1348 and not earlier or later. Plague had existed in parts of Asia for centuries and Europeans had been trading with Asia for many years before 1348. The probable answer is a simple one. Before 1348 Europe had no rats, or rather, not enough rats and not enough people to

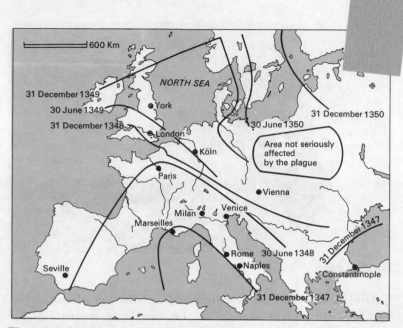

The spread of the Black Death across Europe between 1347 and 1350. The lines show how far the plague had reached by a particular date. Notice how the plague spread in a curve round Europe in a clockwise direction, leaving a plague-free area in the East

make a plague epidemic possible. It may be that there were no rats at all in Europe before about 1200. About that time a few were imported by chance and began to multiply and spread. Medical experts believe that a plague epidemic cannot get going unless the rat community is large enough. Since rats lived mainly on the food humans threw away or stored, the number of rats in any one place could only increase when the number of humans increased. Plague therefore could only break out as an epidemic where quite a large number of humans, and rats, were living close together. Scholars all agree that the number of people in Europe grew quickly in Europe between about 1100 and 1300, so any time after about 1300 there were enough people and rats for a plague epidemic to break out.

88   Plague bacilli, rather like modern 'flu germs, seem to have

had periods when they were fairly mild, followed by short spells of greater violence, or *virulence*, and activity. One of these virulent spells seems to have occurred in central Asia round about 1340 and the active bacilli spread out in all directions; eastward to China, southward to India and westward to Asia Minor (modern Turkey). From there it was only a matter of time before a European trading ship carried the fatal infection into the ports of southern Europe.

The plague lasted in Europe for just over three hundred years. In England it disappeared rapidly after 1666 and it vanished from the continent of Europe over the following sixty years. It is still a mystery why it vanished. Some suggestions that have been put forward are certainly false or incomplete explanations. For England, it is often said that the Great Fire of London wiped out the plague. Certainly the rebuilding of much of central London with new and more rat-resistant houses would have helped, but not all of London was burnt down or rebuilt and in the many suburbs the rats and therefore the plague could have remained.

However, it was not only in central London after the Great Fire that houses were being rebuilt around this time. All over England houses were being improved, rebuilt or newly built and in towns particularly laws were being passed to make them healthier places by, for instance, forbidding people to throw their rubbish into the streets. It may be that the combined effects of better housing and hygiene made England a healthier place.

One simple answer seemed very convincing. Just as a shortage of rats before 1348 made a plague epidemic impossible, so the disappearance of the black rat, killed or chased away by the brown rat, made it impossible for the plague to remain. The plague-carrying flea that lived on the black rat did not much like the brown rat, and anyway the brown rat does not live near humans but out in the woods and fields so its fleas would seldom have the opportunity to bite humans. There is no doubt about the victory of the brown over the black rat but unfortunately for our simple explanation the victory

The Brown Rat

did not occur until about forty years after the plague vanished!

The most recent suggestion is that people began to be infected by a new bacillus, very similar to plague but very much milder. Most people caught this disease when young and this gave them immunity against the plague. Unfortunately it seems that this new bacillus probably reached England a long time after 1670 so the mystery of the plague's disappearance still remains unsolved.

At least we can be fairly certain that it will not come back again, despite recent reports that the black rat is on the increase again! Even if plague were brought into England— the last time was in 1901—doctors, with what they now know about the disease, could prevent it from spreading, as they do with smallpox. If anything is going to kill us off by the million in this century it will either be some vicious and unstoppable brand of 'flu or some man-made horror. In Europe at least, The Black Death is dead!

Things To Do

There may be things that you have read about in this book which you find interesting and would like to know more about. Below there are some suggestions for books you might find it worth while to read or consult. A good historian will always read a lot, but it is not enough just to read, to soak up facts like blotting paper. You must also think a lot. So here, first, are one or two things to think about.

At the very start of this book, I mentioned the dropping of the first atomic bomb on Hiroshima in Japan as the nearest thing to the Black Death in this century. Of course the fact that the Black Death just happened, whilst the bomb was made by humans who took a deliberate decision to drop it makes a big difference. All the same, the results were not so very different. Here is a very short poem written by a victim but survivor of Hiroshima, Kazuo. It could have been written about the Black Death.

> Not on the skin alone
> *Suppurate pustules*.
> Deeper are the heart wounds.
> Will they ever heal?

These words were written by a man who after the dropping of the bomb became 'a common thief who murdered in order to steal'. Can we blame people like Kazuo for their actions?

In the passage below a Japanese history professor explains why he is writing about the Hiroshima bomb. These words sum up for me very well why one should write about and read the history of such horrible things as the Black Death and the Hiroshima bomb. (I have put in italics what I consider the most important words.)

> I would like to tell the facts of the experience [of the bombing of Hiroshima] in a way that people will know about it, not only with their minds but will *feel it with their skin*....I believe

that if Kennedy and Khrushchev [American president and Russian premier] could have seen those people [the victims of Hiroshima] even once, they would feel that they should throw all their nuclear weapons to the bottom of the sea. . . . And that is why the first thing to do is to *help people understand the actual situation of human beings that day*.

Should people who have the power to make decisions which affect others be cool and impersonal when they decide what to do or should they use their imaginations and be influenced by their emotions?

A few years ago a film was made to show what would probably happen if a small atomic bomb was dropped on to an English town. Scenes in the film showed that law and order soon broke down. People started to behave like savages and soldiers had to be used to control the mobs. The film caused a lot of argument and fuss and was banned from public showing. From what you have read about people's behaviour during the Black Death, do you think that the film maker's picture of what happened after the bomb fell is an accurate one. Do you think it was right to prevent people from seeing the film?

If you want to find out more about the Black Death itself, the best book to turn to is *The Black Death* by PHILIP ZIEGLER, published by Penguin. You may find some of this book too detailed and difficult to read but make sure to read Chapter 13, a marvellous imaginary account of the way the Black Death came to one village. There are two useful 'Jackdaws' called *The Black Death* and *Plague and Fire*, both published by Jonathan Cape; the second one describes the great plague of London in 1665. There is also a good description of the 1665 plague in *Plague and Fire*, and *English Life in the Seventeenth Century* has some good pictures. To find out more about villages as they were during the centuries the plague raged in England, read two other Then and Three books, *Medieval Village* by MARJORIE REEVES and *Elizabethan Village* by ROMER HART and ANTHONY FLETCHER. The second gives a splendid picture of the village of Harwell not far from Brightwell, mentioned in this book, and yet another manor owned by the wealthy bishop of Winchester.

Two other Then and Three books can tell you more about subjects briefly mentioned in this book. If you want to know more about town life in Italy, read *Florence in the time of the Medici,* by E.R. CHAMBERLIN. This book also tells you about some of the Renaissance artists, many of whom lived and worked in Florence. For more about the make-believe world and mock wars of the nobles, read *The Medieval*

Tournament by R.J. MITCHELL.

One modern historian has said that every historian 'should get mud on his boots'. He meant that it is not enough just to read books about the past. One should also go and look at the towns and country-side where past events happened. If you live close by, it is worth visiting the various places mentioned in this book. You won't find much sign of a six-hundred-year-old plague in most of them but sometimes local villagers can point out a field which is supposed to have been a special burial ground for the plague. At Eyam there are lots of local stories about the plague and quite a lot still to be seen. Do not miss any opportunity to visit Winchester and make sure you see Bishop Edington's 'temporary' west front of the cathedral and William of Wykeham's magnificent nave. A stone's throw away is Winchester College, the school William founded, to provide education for 'poor scholars'.

The parish registers, such as the one from which the story of the Deanes of Colyton was pieced together, are nowadays usually kept in the County Record Office. Your teacher will probably know where your local record office is. The burials of those who died of plague are often specially marked with a P or an X, especially in town parishes.

Glossary

to absolve, to pardon someone for their sins
abundance, plenty
acre, 4047 square metres
aforesaid, mentioned before
aloe, kind of lily used to make a drug
aqua vitae, brandy or some other spirit
aqueduct, bridge carrying water pipes
bacillus (pl. *bacilli*), tiny vegetable organism which carries disease
bailiff, man employed to run a farm estate when the lord is away
banquet, feast, elaborate meal
benefice, job in the church
bier, stand on which a coffin is carried
calamity, disaster
catalyst, something which causes change without changing itself
commodity, object which is traded (bought and sold)
commutation, changing from payment in goods to a money payment
contado, country district surrounding an Italian town
corrupted, rotted
countenance, face
cupped, to cup was to draw blood from a sick person: doctors in the
    Middle Ages believed this was good for the health
cynical, distrustful and gloomy, contemptuous,
to deign, to condescend, or be prepared to do something
to delve, to dig
demesne, part of the manor estate the lord did not let to tenants
depression, gloom
detriment, harm, damage
diocese, area in church affairs governed by a bishop
distemper, illness
draught ale, beer out of a barrel
94 *epidemic*, disease striking many people at the same time

epizootic, disease striking many animals at the same time

eruption, explosion

to expulse, to expel, get rid of

fanatic, someone who is over-enthusiastic

florin, a gold coin first made in Florence

gill, a quarter of a pint (142 ml.)

hamlet, small village

heretic, person whom the Church considers to follow the wrong form
of Christianity

heriot, payment in money or goods made to the lord of the manor
by the heirs of a tenant who had recently died

Holy Orders, to take Holy Orders is to become a clergyman

hovel, tiny one-room cottage

immunity, 1. a special arrangement which lets a person off a penalty:
2. protection

infallible token, trustworthy sign

layman, ordinary person, not a clergyman

livid, black and blue (like a bruise)

lubber, clumsy or lazy fellow

malady, illness

Malmsey, a kind of wine

manor, large farm estate usually owned by the 'lord of the manor'

massacre, murder of many people at the same time

mead, meadow; (it can also mean a wine made with honey)

means, money

medieval, of the time of the Middle Ages

messuage, plot of land containing a house and garden

Middle Ages, a period of history, roughly from the fifth century to the
fifteenth century AD.

mithridatum, an antidote or medicine against poison

mortar, bowl for crushing things in

to mortify, to inflict pain to avoid falling into temptation

myrrh, gum from a tree, used in medicine

mystic, person who believes religion is mainly to do with thinking

notary, person who draws up legal papers

optimist, someone who hopes for the best, looks on the bright side

pandemic, disease which strikes many people over a wide area at the
same time

parchment, dried skin of a sheep or goat used instead of writing paper

pardoner, man who sold pardons, i.e. forgiveness for sins

parish, church district, or the people in it, cared for by a clergyman

patron, employer or protector

penance, something done to make up for having committed a sin

pessimist, person who takes the gloomy view of things

phantom, ghost or spirit

posse, group of men whose job was to round up criminals

to propagate, to spread

to prove, to establish as true or genuine

pustules, blisters

putrefaction, decay, rottenness

reeve, servant who looked after the day to day affairs of a lord's manor

Renaissance, name given to the spread of learning, painting and other arts in Europe in the 1400s

repulsive, disgusting, off-putting

repute, respectability, good name

to roam, to wander about

rood, quarter of an acre

saffron, kind of autumn crocus from which yellow dye and flavouring are made

scourge, whip used for inflicting pain, or a punishment

scapegoat, someone who is wrongly blamed for something unpleasant

scruple, very small quantity: about 1 gramme

sculpture, figure made by an artist from stone, wood, clay, etc.

seething, bubbling, boiling

serge, strong woollen cloth

sou, coin of small value, like a halfpenny

span, past tense of 'to spin', i.e. to twist wool, cotton etc. into threads

statute, law passed by parliament

stave, long stick

steward, chief servant of a landlord

suckling, baby who is being breast-fed

superstitious, believing things through fear rather than good reason

to suppurate, to ooze

sweltering, sweating

Treacle Venice, a kind of medicine containing honey: the original meaning of 'treacle' is 'medicine against poison'

tumour, infected swelling

venom, poison

virgate, about 30 acres of farmland

virulence, strength of a disease

wake, public holiday

yeoman, well-off farmer